Eugene V. Debs

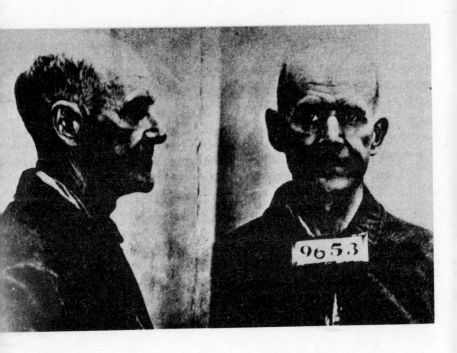

EUGENE VICTOR DEBS, Photograph taken at Atlanta Prison.

WALLS AND BARS

by Eugene Victor Debs

Introduction by Patrick E. Gorman

President of the Debs Foundation, and
International Secretary-Treasurer of the
Amalgamated Meat Cutters and Butcher
Workmen of North America, AFL-CIO

Debs Bibliography by Bernard J. Brommel

1973
Chicago

CHARLES H. KERR & COMPANY

Published in cooperation with the Eugene V. Debs Foundation

Printed in the United States of America

LC   72-87323

ISBN   0-88286-002-X

ACKNOWLEDGEMENT

The Publisher wishes to express the gratitude we feel to Hilton E. Hanna, International Vice President of the Amalgamated Meat Cutters Union and Board member of the Debs Foundation, for his assistance in making this edition of Walls and Bars possible.

Charles H. Kerr & Company

LIST OF ILLUSTRATIONS

TABLE OF CONTENTS

Introduction by Patrick E. Gorman, President of the Debs Foundation, and International Secretary-Treasurer of the Amalgamated Meat Cutters and Butcher Workmen of North America, AFL-CIO.

Debs Bibliography, by Bernard J. Brommel, Northeastern Illinois University, member of the Board of the Debs Foundation.

SYNOPSIS OF CONTENTS.

I.

THE RELATION OF SOCIETY TO THE CONVICT.

My prison experience includes three county jails, one state penitentiary, and one federal prison.—I have no personal grievance to air. Special favors were never accorded me, nor would I accept any.—Introduced to jail life in Chicago, 1894.—Recognized my kinship with prisoners everywhere.—Prison problem is co-related with poverty which is a social disease.—Any of us may go to prison at any time for breaking the law or upholding it.—My spirit was never imprisoned.

II.

THE PRISON AS AN INCUBATOR OF CRIME.

The boy's first offense.—Convicted, manacled and taken to prison.—How he is received and what happens to him.—How he feels about it.— He is thrown into contact with hardened criminals; the degenerating process begins.—A few days later the change is apparent.—He acquires a new vocabulary.—His self-respect begins to wane.—He has taken the first lesson in the school of vice and crime from which he is to graduate as a finished product at the expiration of his term.   III.

I BECOME U. S. CONVICT, No. 9653.

Transferred from Moundsville penitentiary in charge of an United States Marshal and three deputies.—How I was received in Atlanta and my first impressions.—The Bertillon system is applied.—Stripped, bathed and put in prison garb.—In the office of the deputy warden.—My introduction to the warden.—Assigned to duty in the clothing room.—I begin to serve my sentence.

IV.

Sharing the Lot of Les Miserables.

My cell and cell mates.—The prison routine.—Prison food and how it is served.—My first infraction of prison rules; how it resulted and the outcome.—Caged fourteen hours daily.—Getting in touch with my fellow prisoners in the stockade.

V.

Transferred From My Cell to the Hospital.

Mingling with the diseased, the maimed and the infirm.—The drug addicts and their treatment.—Hospital guard clubs a convict.—The blood-covered victim and the dismissal of the guard.—The dying and the dead.—Reading and writing their letters.—My voluntary ministrations to the suffering.—The moral atmosphere changes.

VI.

Visitors and Visiting.

Privileges and the lack of them.—Restrictions upon visits.—A guard sits between the convict and his visitor to overhear.—A state delegation pays me a call.—The curiosity of casual visitors to see me is denied.—My visitors included Melville E. Stone, Samuel Gompers, Lincoln Steffens, Norman Hapgood, Clarence Darrow, and other prominent personages.

VII.

The 1920 Campaign for President.

Unanimous nomination by the New York convention.—The notification committee appears.—Reception in the warden's office.—Addressing the voters through weekly statements issued from prison.—The inmates are enthusiastic and assure the candidate he will carry the prison unanimously.—Receiving the returns on election night in the warden's office.—I concede Harding's election to waiting reporters.

VIII.

A Christmas Eve Reception.

My fellow prisoners spread a bounteous table of their gifts and make me their guest of honor.—President Wilson denies Attorney General Palmer's recommendation for my release, Christmas, 1920.—The beautiful aspect of prison fellowship.—My comment on President Wilson results in the suspension of my writing and visiting privileges, and I am placed incommunicado.—The instant and widespread protest, that followed, forces revocation of the order.

IX.

Leaving the Prison.

Sensational demonstration at parting and agitation of the inmates. Leaving them behind overcame me as with a sense of desertion and guilt.—Pallid faces pressed hard against the bars of that living tomb.—Outside the portals and midway across the reservation, the warden and his deputy stood aghast as there came from the prison a demonstration repeated over and over.—Never had the rules been thus violated at the departure of an inmate.—Tearful, haunted faces, swept by emotion, forgot for the moment hard and forbidding prison rules, giving a last roar of emotion as our auto was lost in the distance.

X.

GENERAL PRISON CONDITIONS.

The guns on the walls.—The clubs in the hands of the guards.—Brutal, stupid and unnecessary rules.—Guards with clubs preside over devotional services.—Inmates at the mercy of prison guards.—Work of convicts grudgingly done.—Stool pigeons play their nefarious part.—The maddening monotomy and its demoralizing results.

XI.

POVERTY POPULATES THE PRISON.

With but few exceptions the poor go to prison.—The moneyless man in court.—The law's delay.—Holding the accused in jail under graft system of petty officials.—In the pillory of a courtroom.—Foulness of county jails and contamination of youthful first offenders.—Perversion of natural sex instincts and resultant vice and immorality.

XII.

CREATING THE CRIMINAL.

How the lack of money presumes guilt in advance of trial.—Poverty the deadly nemesis on the track of accused.—The process of creating the criminal.—The arrest, trial and conviction as now conducted, and the sentence that follows as now served, almost irrevocably doom the victim to physical and moral wreckage.—Why the prison as a reformatory is not only a flat failure, but a promotor of that which it blindly and stupidly attempts to suppress.

XIII.

HOW I WOULD MANAGE THE PRISON.

The civil service farce in relation to the guards.—The prison under control of absent politicians who have never seen it.—How the drug traffic thrives.—Conflicting rules and a dozen petty prisons behind the same walls.—The planless, purposeless and aimless way of doing things.—Robbing the prisoners and starving their families.—The redeeming power of kindness as a substitute for the brutalizing power of cruelty.—The human element actually applied in Atlanta prison and its amazing results.—A challenge to the powers and personalities that control jails, prisons and penitentiaries in the United States.

XIV.

Capitalism and Crime.

Capitalism and crime almost synonymous terms.—Private ownership of the means of the common life at bottom of prison evil.—Capitalism must have prisons to protect itself from the criminals it has created.—Proud of its prisons which fitly symbolize the character of its institutions.—The letter of a convict forty-eight years behind the bars.

XV.

Poverty and the Prison.

Intimate relation between poor-house and prison.—Poverty the common lot of the great mass of mankind.—It is poverty from which the slums, the red light district, the asylums, the jails and prisons are mainly recruited.—No excuse today for widespread poverty.—A barbarous judge recommends re-establishment of the whipping post.—Abolish the social system that makes the prison necessary and populates it with the victims of poverty.

8

XVI.

Socialism and the Prison.

Socialism and prison antagonistic terms.—Socialism will abolish the prison as it is today by removing its cause.—Capitalism and crime have had their day and must go.—The working class to become the sovereign rulers of the world.—The triumph of socialism will mean the liberation of humanity throughout the world.

LEAVING THE PRISON.

XVII.

Prison Labor, Its Effects on Industry and Trade.

Address before the Nineteenth Century Club at Delmonico's, New York City, March 21st, 1899.

XVIII.

Studies Behind Prison Walls.

An article reproduced by the courtesy of its publishers from the Century Magazine for July, 1922.

XIX.

Wasting Life.

Reproduced from The World Tomorrow for August, 1922, by the courtesy of its publishers.

INTRODUCTION

by Patrick E. Gorman

President of the Debs Foundation and Secretary-Treasurer of the Amalgamated Meat Cutters and Butcher Workmen of North America, AFL-CIO

Nearly fifty years ago, Eugene V. Debs in this classic work of his - WALLS AND BARS - issued a clarion call for all who are committed to justice, equality, dignity and opportunity to stand up and be counted against the dehumanizing - indeed barbaric - policies and practices of the prison system of the nation.

In light of the prison violence and outbreaks that have rocked the nation with increasing ferocity in the intervening years and the reaction of the public to them, there seems to be but one logical conclusion, namely: that as a nation, we are still as savage a people as the day Debs first called attention to the atrocities of the prison nearly half a century ago.

Contrast Debs' clearness of vision, depth of insight and intensity of concern for his fellowmen - especially those who find themselves victims of the "class-caste" system and are incarcerated or "liquidated" mainly to appease the sadistic lust of the Power Structure - with the archaic and baronial fulminations of the present occupant of the White House, the 37th President of the United States.

Just recently - in one of his "unscheduled," "unannounced" State of the Nation addresses, the President, in a most fanatical manner, called for the return of the

10

death penalty, outlawed by the U.S. Supreme Court, for certain crimes, primarily against the Establishment. In the latest turn of events, according to the New York Times of March 19, 1973, the President now seeks to abolish insanity as a defense against murder and Federal crimes. Legal experts advise that insanity as defense in such situations has been recognized under varying definitions for over a century.

In the same State of the Nation address, the President likewise made known his intentions to do everything in his power to promote the tightening of regulations and restrictions for many crimes - a good many of which might more correctly be labeled "entrapments."

Under the guise of the so-called "Law and Order" banner, therefore, the Chief Executive endeavors to beguile the gullible and unsuspecting into supporting his Presidential views and policies on crimes and criminal justice. In so doing, the President flies in the face of the preponderance of evidence and prevailing sentiment of professional penologists. They have long contended and still maintain that such harsh programs and policies as advocated by the Chief Executive are distinctly counter productive to the humane rehabilitation of the unfortunate who run afoul of the law.

Under no circumstances can the labor movement remain aloof from the struggle for prison reform. Nor must we allow ourselves to be hoodwinked by the many so-called "Law and Order" groups. We must lose no time in unmasking the hooded one to see who it is that is really crying "wolf."

The President of the United States, for example, in one breath shrilly talks of "Law and Order" and appropriates millions of dollars to the law enforcement agencies of the Nation supposedly to make the streets and highways safe for everyone. In the next moment, however, he pulls a massive coverup by tossing the mantle of executive privilege over the head and shoulders of his chosen aides to prevent them from furnishing urgently needed information to a duly constituted Congressional Committee desperately seeking the facts to make an honest determination in a case of vital significance not only to the "Law and Order" crusade but to the entire Nation.

Under these circumstances, can the cry for "Law and Order" be considered genuine, or must it be seen for what it really is; namely, "class warfare" specifically designed to keep in their place labor and its natural allies - the poor, the oppressed, the Blacks, the American Indian, the Chicanos and other Spanish speaking peoples, the exploited females, the dispossessed youth, peace advocates and other protesters against the status quo?

The most charitable thing that can be said about the exercise of Presidential prerogative in the specific situation in question is that it widens still further the "credibility gap" that has for years existed between the President and the people.

We of labor like those in the forefront of the Civil Rights and Civil Liberties movements must never forget that our very existence is rooted in the bitter soil of injunctions, repressions, manhandling, torture and even death itself at the hands of the Establishment and its backers.

In like manner, we of labor and our fellow dissenters must ever remember that prisons were never established to be palaces for the rich or for law breakers among the high and mighty. Obviously, by their breeding and environment, the "lords" and "ladies" could do no wrong.

If by chance, however, any of them proved to be less than discreet, and were caught infringing on the "rules of the club," they would be tapped on the wrist and possibly even mildly scolded but the "hoosegow" they would never see. Other arrangements would be made for them.

Prisons were designed and established, as Debs discovered during his stay behind the gray walls of the County Jail in Chicago, Woodstock Prison and Atlanta Penitentiary, as horror pens where workers and their allies were dispatched to wait and rot in filth with other workers and dissenters. This torture frequently runs for weeks, months or even years on end until the courts or the system they represent get around to calling whomever remained for hearing and trial or until the inmates had yielded up the ghost and died from frustration, boredom, overcrowding or assault by fellow inmates. In our day the drug menace in its various forms adds another dimension and myriad of problems to the prison life of the poor.

It is not enough to talk about prison reforms in a vacuum. In addition to marching to the State Capitols, City Halls and County Buildings to press home our point about prison reforms in its varied aspects, organized labor has a duty and responsibility to become doers, as well as talkers in the crusade for healthier, more humane prisons.

The prison uprisings that periodically take place all have the same origin, the need to protest against intolerable conditions, and to gain publicity for the demands of inmates that are not heard otherwise. It is apparent that this is the area where the labor movement ought to make its influence felt. The need for a genuine grievance machinery, real negotiations, and lasting concern for the conditions behind the walls and bars, - this is where the experience and concerns of the labor movement can spark a real movement for reform of the horrible, backward and inhuman conditions that are so widespread in American prisons.

The routine of negotiating during an uprising, and then back to the same old conditions that made the uprising inevitable - this vicious circle must be broken and only a systematic and regular and representative negotiating process, supported by the labor movement with its expertise in negotiation and its resources for publicity hold the promise of reform. The workers in prisons need the representation of the labor movements - that is the most logical and most reasonable way out of the present impasse. Harsher laws, as proposed by Nixon and Rockefeller can only lead to further bloodbaths.

Our involvement could include the promotion and conducting of apprenticeship programs to help inmates better prepare themselves for gainful employment when they are returned to society.

In addition, we should:

(1) Take active part in helping to reform penal codes and practices.

(2) Aid inmates in securing better compensation for their work and services.

(3) Form "Voluntary Brigades" to educate the public on the crimes we commit by keeping citizens incarcerated long after they have paid their "debt to society."

(4) Help negotiate wage increases for prison labor whether produced by head or hands.

Let the worker and non-worker alike never lose sight of the fact that here in the U.S.A. the free enterprise system - for better or worse - is still the economic way of life of the nation. So long as this situation prevails it is a foregone conclusion that any who may run afoul of The System and attack property in its various forms will be meted out stiffer penalties than those who assault human beings. In other words, where profits and property rights carry a higher priority than human rights whomever runs head on into the former will certainly suffer the penalty - "to fit the crime."

We of labor have traditionally - and vigorously - opposed so-called "lie detector tests" or other forms of invasion of the private lives and rights of the individual. The mushrooming of types and styles of electronic snooping and "bugging," whether by Government, industry or blackmailers of the private sector, ought to be no less vigorously opposed.

This whole "law and order" farce smacks too much of the tactics employed forty or fifty years ago by the authorities to gag labor and throw its leaders into jail on literally any trumped up charge. At that time it was labor and its natural allies that stood up and challenged the status quo and The System.

The System, of course, was the capitalisitic system - the social economic and political system that built its empire and rose ever higher among the exploiting nations of the world - feasting carrion-like on the broken bones, emaciated bodies and blasted lives of the real producers of wealth - the working slaves and wage earners.

Today probably more than ever before "eternal vigilance is the price of our liberty." Beware, therefore, of "wolves" in sheep's clothing, bikinis, hot pants, "tails," blue jeans or evening gowns, hair pieces, wigs, natural hairdos - or in whatever shape or form they might come.

The informers have been with us always. Over the years, spying and snooping have been perpetual hazards of labor or others who held so-called "unorthodox" or "radical" views.

In the case of our own International Union, for example, the Password was instituted very early in our history. It was introduced as a means of foiling would-be spies, and stooges, in their attempt to "crash" or infiltrate our membership meetings. In those days only legitimate dues paying members were given the Password which was the key to the union hall. The Password was not discontinued by our International Union until after World War II.

It ought to be emphasized that it was a technique of survival that forced workers to flee from city to city changing names, faces, jobs, general appearances not only week by week but frequently day by day. Those heroes of the early years of our union were dubbed "boomer butchers." They were the ones who stirred the hearts of the unorganized and exploited to join their fellow workers in the Amalgamated, The Union of the Broad Shoulders. They stood up to the bosses whenever and wherever the welfare of the workers was concerned.

For their efforts on behalf of their fellow workers, these "boomer butchers" were hunted and tracked down by the labor hating agents of the big packers and their industrial allies.

Labor hating and spying grew to such a lucrative business that so-called detective agencies mushroomed across the country offering their services for "protection" to their commercial and industrial clients. Heading the list of these notorious "Agencies" were the Pinkerton Detective Agency and the Burns Detective Agency.

By 1937, the LaFollette Civil Liberties Committee which was established for the specific purpose of investigating violations of free speech and the rights of labor unearthed evidence that the labor spying and labor wrecking activities of American industries constituted an $80 million a year racket or illegitimate enterprise.

The so-called services of furnishing spies in their various forms to American industry were provided through three principal sources. These were 1) private detective agencies which sell their services to employers at a profit; 2) employers' associations which along with other activities render spying services to their employer members who requisition it; 3) corporations which provide their own spying systems. In addition, spying on workers and their organizations is occasionally performed by the "industrial squads" of various city and state police departments.

Throughout history the dissenters and non-conformists have always been "fair game" for the oppressors and their hirelings. They have always been hounded and hunted, pressured and pursued, by the "palace guard" of the Power Structure. Anyone irreverent enough to "breach the rules of society" - especially if the "crime" is against The Establishment, their heirs or appendages - is forthwith given his come-uppance.

At one time they would be whipped or scourged until their bodies were bathed in blood. In our day they

17

are thrown into the stockades, tortured and literally left to die a slow death in the filth, rubble and molestations of the "big house" "the tomb" "the rock" as these so-called "correctional institutions" are known to the inmates.

Few groups of the nation have been more of a victim of oppression and brutality or bear deeper scars of THE SYSTEM than organized labor. The whole industrial landscape of the nation is strewn with bomb-like craters in labor-management relations. Those who think that the current wave of bugging, blackmailing, espionage and treachery is a new development in the life of the nation will find a rude awakening in store for them if they will but check the pages of the industrial warfare of the U. S. A.

Spying on workers, or any others in the community, advocating what might be called a "different" philosophy than the view held by the rulers has been an "accepted" way of life of the nation literally from its very foundings.

The story of the "witch hunts" and the "burning at the stake" of so-called "heretics" in New England in the early days of the nation, or the lynching and dismemberment of the "uppity" Blacks of the South and the "outlaws" of the West, in what was known as the "wild and wooly" days of the nation are but illustrations of the intolerance of a people whose very existence is rooted in the flight from intolerance in the Old Countries across the sea.

In a similar spirit, and of much longer duration, some of that same savageness and bestiality have been meted out to the labor movement and its natural allies for more than a century.

— — — — — — — — —

Deb's creed as presented in the closing words of his historic Canton, Ohio speech Sunday afternoon, June 16, 1918 sets the tone and stands as an ever present challenge to labor and others who would follow in his footsteps with a determination to help make our community and world better places in which all people may live in justice, dignity and respect. Hear him!

> "Socialism is a growing idea, an expanding philosophy. . . It is the mightiest movement in the history of mankind. The little that I am, the little that I am hoping to be, I owe to the Socialist movement. It has given me my ideas and ideals; my principles and convictions; and I would not exchange them for all of Rockefeller's bloodstained dollars.
>
> It has taught me that ecstacy in the handclasp of a comrade. . .
>
> It has enabled me to hold high communion with you in the great struggle for the better day. . . . . .
>
> to know that I am kin to all that throbs; to be class conscious and to realize that, regardless of Nationality, race, creed, color or sex, every man, every woman who toils renders useful service.
>
> Every member of the working class without an exception, is my comrade, my brother and sister - and that to serve them and their cause is the highest duty of my life."

EUGENE V. DEBS

A SELECTED BIBLIOGRAPHY
by Dr. Bernard J. Brommel,
Northeastern Illinois University, Chicago, Illinois

During his lifetime, Debs delivered over six thousand speeches and wrote approximately three thousand items for publication in newspapers, journals and books. No one ever kept a record of these assignments which Debs gladly performed for the sake of the working man. He once commented that he served as the "tongue of the working class" and would continue to speak out until the workers gained fundamental rights.

Debs' ideas regarding prison reform appeared in various short references in his speeches and writings. After his prison sentence following the Pullman Strike in 1894, he understood many of the problems faced by prisoners and thereafter followed closely issues related to prison reform.

Items in this bibliography which focus upon Debs' ideas about prisons or reflect on his experiences as a prisoner have been marked in the outer margin with an asterisk. Remember this is a selected bibliography which includes a wide cross section of works by Debs and works about Debs. Copies of all of these works can be found in Debs MS at the Indiana State University Library, Terre Haute, Indiana. The special collection is housed in the new library, a block away from the restored Eugene V. Debs' Home which welcomes visitors.

EUGENE V. DEBS: A SELECTED BIBLIOGRAPHY

WORKS BY DEBS

Debs, Eugene V. *Address to the Jury and Statement to the Court.* Chicago, National Office of the Socialist Party, n. d.

. "The American Labor Party," *Socialist World,* (January, 1925).

. *The American Movement.* Terre Haute, Indiana, Standard Publishing Co., 1904.

. "Appeals to Save Sacco and Vanzetti, Calls upon American Labor to Make Nationwide, United Protest in Behalf of Victims," *American Appeal* (May 29, 1926), 1 - 2.

. *Arouse, Ye Slaves: An Address.* Chicago, Social Democratic Party of America, n. d.

. "Bryan and the Commoner," *Appeal to Reason,* (March 30, 1907), 1.

. *But Two Parties and But One Issue.* Opening Speech the Campaign of 1912 at Riverview Park, Chicago, Illinois, June 16, 1912, Chicago, Allied Printing, 1912.

. *Candidate for President.* Address of Acceptance. New York, Jewish Socialist Federation, 1912.

. *Canton Speech.* Chicago, Socialist Party of the United States, n. d. (Actually delivered on June 18, 1918 in Canton, Ohio.)

. "The Cartoonist and the Social Revolution." Article in Ryan Walker *et al., The Red Portfolio: Cartoons Socialism,* n. p., n. d.

. *Champion of the American Working-Class.* New York, City Committee of the Socialist Party of Greater New York, 1920.

. *Childhood.* Terre Haute, Indiana, n. p., n. d.

. *The Children of the Poor.* Chicago, National Office of the Socialist Party, ca. 1912.

. "The Church and the Revolution," *Debs Magazine* (April 1922), 12.

. "Civilization of the Whipping Post: Delaware's Imperishable Infamy," *Coming Nation,* February 10, 1912), 7.

. *Class Unionism.* Speech delivered at South Chicago, November 24, 1905. Revised by the author. Reissued October 1909. Chicago, Charles H. Kerr and Co., n. d.

. "Confederation of Labor Organizations Essential to Labor's Prosperity," *American Journal of Politics.* (n. d.), 63 - 71.

. *Craft Unionism.* Speech delivered at Chicago, November 23, 1905. Revised by the Author and reissued October 1909. Chicago, Charles H. Kerr and Co., n. d.

. "The Crime of Craft Unionism," *International Socialist Review,* (February 1911), 465.

. *The Crying Need of the Day.* Chicago, Socialist Party, ca. 1920.

* . "Current Comment: Chicago's Filthy Jail," *Debs Magazine,* (November 1922), 4.

. "Current Comment: Church for Peace," *Debs Magazine,* (November 1922), 4 - 5.

. *Danger Ahead for the Socialist Party in Playing the Game of Politics.* Chicago, Charles H. Kerr and Co., n. d.

. "Darkness and Dawn," [Review of a book titled *Darkness and Dawn* by George Allan England.] Published as a leaflet, Boston, Maynard and Co., n. d.

. *Day of the People.* N. p., Socialist Party, n. d.

. "Debs and Longuet," *Debs Magazine,* (December 1922), 3 - 5, 14 - 15.

* . *Debs and the War.* His Canton speech and his trial in the Federal Court at Cleveland, September 1918. Chicago, National Office of the Socialist Party, n. d., 1 - 64.

. "Debs Announces His Decision," *Debs Magazine,* (October 1922), 5 - 7, 15.

. "Debs' Challenge," *Debs Magazine,* (January 1923), 3 - 4.

. "Debs Reply to Roosevelt," *Appeal to Reason,* (May 1, 1909), 1.

* . "Divine Service Under the Guards' Clubs," *New York American,* June 18, 1922.

. "Editorial," *National Ripsaw,* (October 1916), 3.

. "The End of Craft Unionism," *Debs Magazine,* (October 1922), 3.

. "Eugene Field: Poet and Humanist," *Welcome News,* (November, 1939), 8. [A reprint from *Pearson's Magazine,* (September 1917.]

. *Excerpts from a Speech Delivered at Grand Central Palace, New York.* New York, United Workers of America, Committee of Action, n. d.

. "Fantine in Our Day," *The Call Magazine,* (February 3, 1918), 1.

. *The Federal Government and the Chicago Strike.* Terre Haute, Indiana. The Standard Publishing Co., 1904.

. *The Fight for Liberty.* Chicago, Socialist Party, n. d.

. *Fight to the Last!* An address delivered [at] . . . Labor Lyceum, March 19, 1910.

. *The Forbidden Speech.* Philadelphia, Socialist Party, n. d. Forbidden the use of the largest hall in town by the police, Debs delivered this speech at the Labor Lyceum, Sunday, October 11, 1908.

* . "From Woodstock to Boise," *Appeal to Reason,* (November 23, 1907), 1.

. "George Allan England's 'Air Trust,' an_ Appreciation," St. Louis, Missouri, *The National Ripsaw,* n. d. [leaflet]

. *The Growth of Socialism.* Chicago, Charles H. Kerr and Co., n. d.

*   . "Help Debs' Appeal," n. p., n. d. [Says send all money to Oliver C. Wilson, Chicago, Illinois. Internal: proof: Debs 62 at time written: ca. 1917]

. *The Heritage of Debs: The Fight Against War*. Chicago, Socialist Party National Headquarters, 1935.

. *Historic Labor Battle*. Philadelphia, Socialist Party of Philadelphia, 1910.

. "How I Became a Socialist. A Story of the Great A. R. U. Strike . . . and Deb-its and Credits." *Debs Freedom Monthly*, (October 1921), 3 - 4, 13, 22.

. "How I Became a Socialist," *New York Comrade*, (April 1902).

. "The Indictment of Our Leaders," April 1918. [No. 16 of the Series of Organization Leaflets issued monthly by National Office of the Socialist Party, Chicago, Illinois.]

. *Industrial Unionism*. An address delivered at Grand Central Palace, New York, Sunday, December 10, 1905. Chicago, Charles H. Kerr and Co., n. d. Also Published by New York Labor News Co., n. d.

. "Ingersoll," *The Melting Pot*, (April 1915), 14 - 15.

*   . "Inside Prison Walls," *New York American*, June 11, 1922.

. "I Oppose Dictatorship," A Message from the Founder of the Socialist Party. New York, n. p., n. d.

. "The International March to Victory," *Debs Magazine*, (December 22), 8.

. *The Issue.* Chicago, Charles H. Kerr and Co., n. d.

. "John Brown: History's Greatest Hero," *Appeal to Reason,* (November 23, 1907), 1.

. "Labor in Politics," *Appeal to Reason,* (January 18, 1908).

. "Lessons in Capitalism," *Debs Magazine,* (March 1923).

. *Letter of Acceptance.* New York, Socialist Party, 1912; 1916.

. *A Letter Regarding Industrial Panics in the United States.* Chicago, Federation of Labor, 1903.

. "A letter to John D. Rockefeller," *Sunday Chronicle,* (June 20, 1897).

. Liberty. Speech delivered at Battery D., Chicago, on release from Woodstock Jail, November 22, 1895. Terre Haute, Indiana, n. p., 1896.

. "Lincoln—Champion of Labor," *Debs Magazine,* (February 1922).

. "Lincoln Living and Dead," *Socialist World* (March 1923).

. "Lion Hearted Russia," *Debs Freedom Monthly,* (November 1921).

. "Looking Backwards," Appeal to Reason, Girard, Kansas, (November 23, 1907).

. "The Martyred Apostles of Labor," The New Time. (February 1899).

. "A Message from Debs," *Rand School Call,* (1902).

. "The Million Voiced Protest," *Appeal to Reason,* (February 9, 1907).

. *Die Mission der Social Demokratischen Partei.* New York, Social Democratic Party of New York, n. d.

. *The Mission of the Socialist Party.* Chicago, National Committee of the Socialist Party, n. d.

. *Motherhood and Suffrage.* Racine, Wisconsin, n. p., n. d. Also published by Terre Haute, Indiana, Standard Publishing Co., n. d.; Chicago Charles H. Kerr and Co., n. d.

. "Murder in the First Degree," editorial, *National Rip-Saw,* (October 1916).

. "The Negro: His Present Status and Outlook," *The Intercollegiate Socialist,* (April-May 1918).

. "The Negro: His Present Status and Outlook," *Public Ownership,* (June 15, 1918).

. "The Negro Question," *American Labor Journal,* Butte, Montana, July 1903.

. *The Negro Workers.* Address delivered Tuesday, October 30, 1923, at Commonwealth Casino, 135th Street and Madison Avenue, New York City. New York, the Emancipation Publishing Co., n. d.

. "Never Be a Soldier," *Appeal to Reason,* (August 1915).

. "Our Party—Its Past and Its Future," *Socialist World* (June 1924).

. Outlook for the Future: The World is Waiting. (A speech delivered at the 21st Convention of Socialist Party, Local Cuy County, Cleveland, Ohio, 1922).

. "The Pickets at the Gate," *The Birth Control Review,* (December 1918) [Article written for M. Sanger and her magazine.]

. "A Plea for Solidarity," International Socialist Review, (March 1914).

. "Political Appeal to American Workers." Opening speech of the National Campaign at Riverview Park, Chicago, June 16, 1912. [Same speech as "But Two Parties and But One Issue," different title and publisher.](Charles H. Kerr and Co., Chicago, n. d.)

*   . *Prison Labor Address* delivered before Nineteenth Century Club at Delmonico's, New York City, March 21, 1899. Published by E. V. Debs and Company, Terre Haute, Indiana in *Progressive Thought,* (April 1899).

. "Public Speaking," *Debs Magazine* (December 1922). [Advertisement of a course to make young socialists speak "like a Debs."]

. "Pullman Greets Debs Again," *Debs Magazine,* (April 1923).

. "Recollections of Ingersoll," *Pearson's Magazine,* (April 1917).

. *Reply to John Mitchell.* Terre Haute, Indiana, Standard Publishing Company, 1904.

. "The Reward of 'Paytriotism'," *Socialist World,* (June 1922).

28

. *Revolutionary Unionism*. Speech delivered at Chicago, November 25, 1905. Revised by the author and reissued September 1909. Chicago, November 25, 1905. Revised by the author and reissued September 1909. Chicago, Charles H. Kerr and Co., n. d.

. "The Right to Work," *Debs Magazine* (September 1922).

. *Riley, Nye and Field: Personal Notes and Recollections*. Terre Haute, Indiana, n. p., n. d.

. "Roosevelt and His Regime," Appeal to Reason, (April 20, 1907).

* . *Sacco and Vanzetti Are Innocent Men; They shall Not be Murdered!* n. p., n. d. [Copy in Debs' MS, Indiana State University, Terre Haute, Indiana.]

. "The Secret of Efficient Expression," *Distinguished Contemporary Orators and Lecturers,* Compiled by University of Wisconsin, [c. 1919]. [Also reprinted in *Coming Nation,* July 8, 1911.]

. "Significance of Labor Day." *Arena,* (October 1895).

. "Slavery or Solidarity," *Debs Magazine,* (May 1922).

. "The Social Democracy," *New Time,* (August 1897).

. *The Socialist Party and the Working Class*. Chicago, Charles H. Kerr and Co., n. d. Opening address as candidate for President, Indianapolis, September 1, 1904; also, published by Terre Haute, Indiana, Standard Publishing Co., 1904.

. *Social Unrest and World Ideals*. New York, n. p., 1907. [In commemoration of the founding of the Brooklyn Labor Lyceum, 1822—1907.]

. *Souvenir Volume Golden Wedding Anniversary.* [Banquet for Debs' parents, Marguerite and Daniel Debs,] 1899.

. *Speech as Reported by E. R. Sterling.* Delivered at Nimisilla Park, Canton, Ohio. Sunday afternoon, June 18, 1918: Speech as charged in the indictment. N. p., n. d.

. "Speech Delivered at Columbia Exposition in Chicago on August 30, 1893," *Fireman's Magazine,* (October 1893). [Speech requested by Henry Demarest Lloyd.]

. *Speech Delivered at Nimisilla Park,* Canton, Ohio, June 18, 1918. N. p., n. d.

. *Speeches of Eugene V. Debs and Daniel DeLeon.* New York, New York Labor News Co., n. d. Reprint of Debs' speech delivered at the first Convention of the Industrial Workers of the World, 1905.

. "Speech of Eugene V. Debs to Industrial Workers of the World," *Proceedings of the First Convention, Chicago, June 27—July 8, 1905.*

. *The Speeches of Eugene V. Debs, Social Democratic Candidate for President, and Professor George D. Herron. . .* [Delivered at formal opening of National Campaign, at Central Music Hall, Chicago, September 29, 1900] Chicago, Social Democratic Party, n. d.

. "Speech to Steel Workers, November 24, 1905." *Appeal to Reason,* (December 16, 1905).

* . "The Story of a Convict," *The Call Magazine,* (March 23, 1918).

. "The Struggle for Freedom," *Debs Magazine,* (March 1923).

. "This is America," *Debs Magazine,* (July 1922).

* . "Thru Prison Walls His Voice Still Calls," *Debs Freedom Monthly,* (August 1921).

. "Tom Mooney Sentenced to Death," *International Socialist Review,* (April 1917).

. "To Our Russian Comrades!" Brooklyn, New York, Socialist Publication Society, November 7, 1918, [pamphlet].

. *To the People of the East Side.* Address delivered at demonstration on October 13, 1908. New York, Eugene V. Debs Headquarters, 9th Congressional District, n. d.

. *To the Women of America.* Chicago, National Office of the Socialist Party. [1920?]

. "To the Woman Voter," [Campaign leaflet] Terre Haute, Indiana, Allied Printing, 1920.

. "Toward the Sunset," Culturist Magazine, 1904.

. "The Truth About Bryan," *The American Monthly,* no date on this clipping in Marguerite Debs Cooper Ms.

. Susan B. Anthony: A Reminiscence," *The Socialist Woman,* (January 1909).

. Unionism and Socialism: *A Plea for Both.* Terre Haute, Indiana, Standard Publishing Co., 1904. 44 pp. [Later published in a longer 65-page edition by Charles Kerr and Co., Chicago]

. *Unity and Victory* Speech . . . delivered before the State Convention of the A.F. of L., at Pittsburg, Kansas, August 12, 1908. Chicago, Charles H. Kerr and Co., n. d.

. "The University Oratorical Report," *The Coming Nation,* (July 8, 1911).

. *A Vision of the Future.* N. p., n. d.

. "The Voice of Debs," Debs Magazine, (August 1922).

. The Voice of Labor. Extracts from address to the jury at his trial in Cleveland, Ohio. Chicago, National Office of the Socialist Party, [1920].

* . Walls and Bars. Chicago, Socialist Party, 1927.

. What Did Debs Say— [Quotes from Debs' Anti-War remarks at Canton.] Chicago, Debs Freedom Conference, n. d.

. "Why Railroaders Should be Socialists," [No. 10 *Appeal to Reason* Leaflets, Girard, Kansas], n. d.

. "Woman," *Debs Magazine,* (March, 1922), 9. Also Debs published a leaflet by same name years earlier in Terre Haute, Indiana, n. d.

. *Woman—Comrade and Equal.* Chicago, National Office of the Socialist Party, [1912].

. *Woman—Comrade and Equal.* Girard, Kansas, *The Progressive Woman,* n. d.

. "A Word to Our Friends," *Debs Magazine,* (February 1923).

A Word to Young People. Fitchburg, Massachusetts, National Office IPSL, n. d.

. "Working Class Politics," Speech in Riverview Park, Chicago, September 18, 1910. Reported by William Cherney, *International Socialist Review,* (November 1910).

. *The World's Record.* Judicial edition of the Appeal to Reason, (April 12, 1912).

. You Railroad Men. Chicago, n. p., n. d.

ARTICLES AND BOOKS ABOUT DEBS

*Aldred, Guy A. *Convict 9653: America's Vision-Maker.* Glasgow, n. p., n. d.

"The America of Debs," *Eugene V. Debs Centennial.* New York, Socialist Society, 1956.

"Application for Pardon of Eugene V. Debs, December 23, 1921. Letter from Attorney General H. M. Daugherty and President Harding, Washington, Government Printing Office, 1922.

Baker, A. S. "Debs Co-operative Commonwealth," *Outlook,* LVI (July 3, 1897).

Beckwith, H. W. *History of Vigo and Parke Counties.* Chicago, H. H. Hill and N. Iddings Publishers, 1880.

Bell, Daniel. *The End of Ideology.* (Glencoe, Illinois, 1960.)

Bell, Daniel, Egert, Donald D. and Persons, Stow, *Socialism in American Life.* (Princeton, 1952.)

Benson, Allen L. "The Socialist Candidates," *Pearson's Magazine,* August 1912.

Bicknell, George. "Eugene V. Debs at Home," *Twentieth Century Magazine,* II (1910).

"Blind," *The New Republic,* December 17, 1919.

Bobspa, David. "My Big Brother Gene," *The New Justice,* April 1, 1919.

Bowers, Claude. *My Life.* New York, Simon and Schuster, 1962.

Bradsby, H. C. *History of Vigo County.* Chicago, S. B. Nelson and Co., 1891.

Brommel, Bernard J. "Debs' Cooperative Commonwealth Movement in America," *Labor History,* Fall Issue, 1972.

. "Eugene V. Debs and Negro Rights," *Congressional Record - Senate* October 17, 1967.

. "The Pacifist Speechmaking of Eugene V. Debs," *The Quarterly Journal of Speech,* April 1966, Volume LII.

. "Eugene V. Debs: The Agitator as Speaker," *Central States Speech Journal,* Winter Issue, 1969.

Burns, Edward McNall. *David Starr Jordan.* Stanford, California, Stanford University Press, 1953.

"The Campaign Before Us," *The Bulletin,* March 1916.

"Calls It Murder: E. V. Debs Declares Sheriff and His Men are Criminals," Chicago Chronicle, September 11, 1897.

Cannon, James P. *The Debs Centennial.* New York, Pioneer Publishers, 1956.

. "The Revolutionary Heritage of Eugene V. Debs," *Labor Defender* [Debs Memorial Number], December 1926.

"The Case of Mr. Debs," *Much Ado,* November 15, 1920.

Caylor, George N. "That Was Debs" [Originally typed May 21, 1943. Retyped with slight changes and additions, May 4, 1960.]

Cherney, William. "Working Class Politics," *International Socialist Review,* November 1910.

Claessens, August. *Eugene V. Debs.* New York, Rand School Press, 1946.

Coldwell, Joseph M. *My Life in Prison with Debs.* Workers Party of America, n. d. [An advertisement of a lecture.]

Coleman, McAlister. *Eugene V. Debs, A Man Unafraid.* New York, Greenberg Publishers, 1930.

⸱ "Eugene Debs, the Beloved," *Pioneers of Freedom.* New York, Vanguard Press, 1929.

"Color Live Talk. Railway Union Discusses the Admission of Negroes," *Chicago Dispatch,* June 6, 1894.

Commons, John R., *et al. History of Labor in the United States.* New York, Macmillan Co., 1918.

Condo, Samuel S. *Memorial Lecture on Eugene V. Debs.* Marion, Indiana, Published by Samuel Condo, n. d.

"Conviction of Debs," *Public,* September 21, 1918.

Crellman, James, "America's Trouble Makers," *Pearson's Magazine,* July 1908.

Cummings, M. "Eugene Debs in Cincinnati," poem, *World Tomorrow,* March 1926.

"Crimes of Carnegie: E. V. Debs Protests against Condoning Crime in Name of Philanthropy," *New York People,* April 7, 1901.

Darrow, Clarence. *Story of My Life.* New York, Scribner and Co., 1932.

"Debs Aids Miners," *Miner's Magazine,* October 29, 1908.

"Debs. The Apostle of Failure," *American Federationist,* September 1908.

"Debs' Appeal," *Outlook,* October 17, 1908.

*"Debs Asserts Charge in Indictment is False," *Indianapolis News,* November 25, 1912.

"Debs Censored by the Ministers," *The Miners Magazine,* December 23, 1909.

*"Debs Defies Laws, Thousands Laud Him, First Public Utterance Since Release," *New York Times,* November 27, 1922.

*Debs Defies U. S. Policy," *Chicago Tribune,* November 27, 27, 1922.

"Debs Centennial Issue," *The Socialist Call,* October, 1955.

*"Debs Indicted in Kansas Court," *Terre Haute Tribune,* November 24, 1912.

"Debs—the Living Link," *Current Literature,* XLV (June 1908).

*"Debs Pardon Refused," *The Independent,* February 12, 1921.

"Debs Shows U. S. Is Controlled by Bosses," [campaign leaflet], Terre Haute, Indiana, Allied Printing, 1920.

Debs, Theodore. "The War and the Workers," *Debs Magazine,* June 1922.

Eastman, Max. "Greek Drama in Cleveland: The Trial of Eugene V. Debs," *Heroes I Have Known.* New York, Simon and Schuster, 1942.

Ehrmann, Max. "Eugene V. Debs," *Pearson's Magazine,* XXXIX (June 1918).

. *The Journal of Max Ehrmann.* Boston, Bruce Humphries, Inc., 1932.

. "Eugene V. Debs as Orator," *Saturday Spectator,* August 19, 1907.

"Eugene Debs' Freilossung." *Volkstimme,* February 8, 1922. Frankfort on the Main, Germany.

Eugene V. Debs; The Man and His Work. Terre Haute, Indiana, n. p., n. d. Comments on Debs by John Swinton, Frank McPhillips, Rev. Frank De Witt Talmadge, Alfred Russell Wallace, Eugene Field, Frederic August Bartholdi, Horace Traubel and James Whitcomb Riley.

"Few Facts, Figures and Statements Concerning Socialism, A," [Leaflet] 1916.

"Free Scholarship!" *Debs Magazine,* July 1922. [Advertisement of scholarship honoring Debs.]

Flynn, Elizabeth Gurley. *Debs and Dennis: Fighters for Peace.* New York, New Century Publishers, 1950.

. *Debs, Haywood, Ruthenberg.* New York, Workers Library Publishers, 1939.

Foner, Phillip S. *Labor Movement in the United States.* New York, International Publishers, 1955.

Fritchman, Stephen H. *Eugene V. Debs.* Los Angeles, n. p., n. d. An address delivered at the First Unitarian Church of Los Angeles, March 22, 1953.

Fyfe, H. "Religion of Eugene Debs," *World Tomorrow,* IX (December 1926).

"Gene Debs' Generosity Used to Victimize Him," *Christian Socialist,* February 1, 1913.

Ghent, U. U. "Eugene V. Debs." *Dictionary of American Biography.* New York, Scribner, 1943. V.

Ginger, Ray. *The Bending Cross, A Biography of Eugene Victor Debs.* New Brunswick, New Jersey, Rutgers University Press, 1949.

Goldberg, Harvey, ed. *American Radicals: Some Problems and Personalities.* New York, Monthly Review Press, 1957.

Golden, Harry. *Carl Sandburg.* Cleveland and New York, The World Publishing Co., 1961.

Harris, Frank. *Pastels of Men.* New York, Pearson's Library, 1919.

*"Harding Frees Debs. No Restoration of Rights," *New York Times,* December 24, 1921.

"Hater of Law and Order," *Harpers Weekly,* XLV (June 20, 1901).

Hancock, Lee. "Paints a Picture of Debs in Cleveland News," *The Miners Magazine,* October 29, 1908.

Hesseltine, William B. *The Rise and Fall of Third Parities,* Washington, D. C., Public Affairs Press, 1948.

High, Fred. "Are We Losing Our Liberty? Is the Incarceration of Eugene V. Debs an Act of Statesmanship? Is Free Speech Banished?" *The Billboard,* Lyceum and Chautauqua Department, August 30, 1919.

Holbrook, Steward H. *Dreamers of the American Dream.* New York, Doubleday and Co., Inc., 1957.

Hollingsworth, J. H. "What His Neighbors Say of Him," n.p., 1913.

Holmes, John Haynes. "Debs—Lover of Men," *Unity*, November 15, 1926. A journal edited by Holmes for the "Religion of Democracy."

Hudson, Hoyt H. "The Debs Decision and the General Strike," *The New Justice*, April 1, 1919.

Hunter, Robert. "A Boy's Estimate of Eugene V. Debs." Unpublished essay. October 25, 1912.

Hurt, Walter. *An Introduction to Eugene V. Debs.* Williamsburg, Ohio, Progress Publishing Co. [ca. 1915].

. "Debs and Sullivan," *The Social Builder*, May 1918.

"Interesting Election Results," *Current Literature*, December 1908.

*"Jail Doors Forced Open by Labor's Two Year Fight," *New York Call*, December 24, 1921.

Journal of the House of Representative of the State of Indiana, Fifty-Fourth Session of the General Assembly. Indianapolis, Wm. B. Burford, Contractor Printer, 1865. Covers Debs' career as a democratic member of this assembly.

Karsner, David. *Debs His Authorized Life and Letters.* New York, Boni and Liveright, 1919.

. "Debs in 1920," *Socialist Review*, June 1920.

. *Talks With Debs in Terre Haute.* New York, *New York Call*, 1922.

Karson, Marc. *American Labor Unions and Politics 1900— 1918.* Carbondale, Illinois, Illinois University Press, 1958.

Keller, Helen. "Wise Fools in High Places," *The Protest,* May 1919.

Kipnis, Ira. *The American Socialist Movement: 1897—1912.* New York, Columbia University Press, 1952.

Kopelin, Louis. *The Life of Debs.* Girard, Kansas, Appeal to Reason, n. d.

* *The Law of the Debs Case: Constitutional Construction by the Supreme Court,* New York, National Civil Liberties Union, n. d.

Lecture Tour of E. V. Debs: Season of 1905—1906. Terre Haute, Indiana, Bureau of American Labor Lyceum, 1905.

"Lecture Tour Outline of Eugene V. Debs and Mrs. O'Hare Covering the Continent," *National Rip-Saw,* June 1914.

LePrade, Ruth, ed. *Debs and the Poets.* Introduction by Upton Sinclair, Pasadena, California, Published by Sinclair, *ca.* 1919.

* *Liberty.* Chicago, Published by the Debs Freedom Conference, n. d. Articles about Debs by Hugh Robert Orr, Bertha Hale White, Celia Rotter, Sophia Vera Rodrigues, Oliver C. Wilson.

London, Jack. *The Dream of Debs: A Story of Industrial Revolt.* Chicago, Charles H. Kerr. n. d.

*Macy, John. "Convict No. 9653," *The Freeman,* March 23, 1921.

*Magnes, Rabbi Judah L. "America's Only Saint," *Debs Freedom Monthly,* November 1921.

Manning, Thomas G. *The Chicago Strike of 1894.* New York, Henry Holt and Co., 1960.

Marky, Alexander. "Saving the Life of 'Gene' Debs," *Pearson's Magazine.* October 1924.

Martin, John Hartlow, "Voices of Protest: E. V. Debs," *Indiana: An Interpretation.* New York, Alfred A. Knopf, 1947.

McFeely, Otto, "Campaigning with Debs," *Wilshire's Magazine,* December, 1908.

McKinney, Martha. "Early Schools in Terre Haute Up to 1889—from unpublished notes of W. H. Wiley." Unpublished thirteen page Ms. on file at Fairbanks Library, Terre Haute, Indiana.

Mencken, H. L. "Slaying the Dragon," *The Call Magazine,* October 30, 1921.

Miller, Martin H. "A Tribute to a Great American." Speeches given at the Debs Centennial Dinner, November 5, 1955, Terre Haute.

"Minutes of City Teachers Institute 1867, 1868, 1869, 1870," Vault: School Administration Building, Terre Haute, Indiana.

"Minute Men Disbanded," *Debs Freedom Monthly,* September 1921.

*Moore, Sam, "Eugene Victor Debs, The Superman - a Close-up view of Him," n. p. n. d., Debs Ms., Indiana State University Library, Terre Haute. [Also signed Convict No. 22. Moore, a black, was reformed by Debs' kindness and example.]

Morais, Herbert M., and William Cahn. *Gene Debs the Story of a Fighting American.* New York, International Publishers, 1948.

Morgan, H. Wayne. *Eugene V. Debs: Socialist for President.* New York, Syracuse University Press, 1962.

Napiere, Leonine. "Debs and the Woman's Movement," *The Birth Control Review,* December 1918.

"The National Socialist Convention of 1912," *International Socialist Review,* XII (June 1912).

Nearing, Scott. *The Debs Decision.* New York, Rand School of Social Science, 1919.

Nissenson, Aaron, Song of Man, *A Novel Based Upon the Life of Eugene V. Debs.* New Haven, Connecticut, Whittier Books, 1964.

Oakey, C. C. *History of Greater Terre Haute and Vigo County.* Chicago, Lewis Publishing Co., 1908.

Old Seminary Folder. Vigo County Historical Society, 1411 South Sixth Street, Terre Haute, Indiana. n. d.

Oneal, James. *Militant Socialism.* St. Louis, National Rip-Saw Publishing Co., 1912.

Owsley, F. L., O. P. Chitwood, and H. C. Nixon. "Social and Economic Friends—The Counter Organization of Labor," *A Short History of the American People, 1865—1947.* Vol. II, New York, D. Van Nostrand Co., 1948.

Painter, Floy Ruth. *That Man Debs and His Life Work.* Bloomington, Indiana, Graduate Council, Indiana University, 1929.

Passos, John Dos. "Lover of Mankind," [Debs] from "U. S. A. from the 42nd Parallel," *American Literature Survey*, ed. Milton R. Stern and Seymour L. Gross. New York, The Viking Press, 1962.

"The People's Nominee on Real Issues!" N. p., 1920.

Pinkerton, William J. *Debs' Treachery to the Working Class*. Chicago, 1911.

Political Guide for the Workers. Socialist Party Campaign Book, 1920. Chicago, Socialist Party of the United States, 1920.

"Portrait," *Chautauqua*, XXXI (April 1900), 9.

"Portrait," *Chautauqua*, XXXIX (June 1904), 20.

"Portrait," *McClure*, XXIII (June 1904).

"Portrait," *Review of Reviews*, XXI (June 1900).

"Portrait," *Review of Reviews*, XXX (August 1904).

*"Prison Release," *New York Call*, January 14, 1922.

Program Philomathean Library Club, July 1, 1869. Files Vigo County Historical Society, Terre Haute, Indiana.

"Railroad Labor," *Fifth Annual Report of the Commissioner of Labor*. Washington, D.C., 1890.

*"Rejoicing Sweeps Prison When Debs is Ordered Freed," *New York Call*, December 24, 1921.

Records Department, Vigo County Court House, Terre Haute, Indiana.

Reed John. "With Gene Debs on the Fourth," *Liberator*, September 1918.

Report on the Chicago Strike, 1894. Washington, D. C., Government Printing Office, 1895.

Resolution on Release of Eugene V. Debs and Other Political Prisoners. Chicago, Debs Amnesty Committee, n. d.

"Responses by Visiting and Resident Comrades Including 'Our Gene'," *An Evening in Girard.* Girard, Kansas, n. p. to Appeal Press, 1908.

Reynolds, Stephen Marion. "Debs at Home: An Appreciation of Eugene V. Debs," Terre Haute, Indiana, Bureau of American Labor Lyceum, n. d.

Riley, James Whitcomb. "About Debs." Poem reprinted in many newspapers and articles. Single copies of it in Debs Ms at Tamiment, n. p., n. d.

"The Rip-Saw Offers Eugene V. Debs for Lectures," *National Rip-Saw,* St. Louis, 1914.

Rogers, Bruce, ed. *Debs: His Life Writings and Speeches.* Girard, Kansas, Appeal to Reason, 1908.[Biographical section by Stephen M. Reynolds.]

Salutski, I. B. *Yudahin Viktor Debs: Zein Leben, Schriften and Redes.* New York, Debs Ferteidigunge Fond, 1919.

Schlesinger, Arthur M., ed. *Writings and Speeches of Eugene V. Debs.* New York, Hermitage Press, Inc., 1948.

Schnittkind, Henry T. *The Story of Eugene Debs.* Boston, National Educational Committee, Independent Workmens Circle, 1929.

"Seidel and the Socialist Dissensions," *Current Literature,* LIII (June, 1912).

Shannon, David A. "Eugene V. Debs Conservative Labor Editor," *Indiana Magazine of History,* XLVII (December 1951).

. *The Socialist Party of America.* New York, The Macmillan Co., 1955.

Shipley, Maynard. "Ten Reasons Why Debs Should Be Sent to Congress," n. p., 1916.

*"Soap-Box Jail," editorial, *New York Times,* February 3, 1921.

"Social Democratic Party's Appeal," *Independent,* LVII (October 13, 1902).

"Social Democratic Party," *Independent,* LII (August 23, 1900).

Social Democracy Red Book. [Campaign Handbook 1900.] Terre Haute, Indiana, Debs Publishing Co.; 1900.

"Socialist Ideals," *Arena,* XL (November 1908).

"Socialist Party Appeal," *Independent,* LXV (October 15, 1908).

"Socialist Party Appeal," *Independent,* LXXIII (October 24, 1912).

"Socialist Party Platform," Chicago, Party Headquarters, J. Mahlon Barnes, Campaign Manager, n. p., 1912. [Leaflet.]

"The Socialist Showing," *The Nation,* December 3, 1908.

"The Socialist Vote," *Literary Digest,* November 23, 1912.

Schorer, Mark. *Sinclair Lewis An American Life.* New York, McGraw Hill and Co., 1961.

Steffens, Lincoln *Autobiography,* New York, Harcourt, Brace Co., 1931.

"Eugene V. Debs on What the Matter Is in America and What to Do About It," *Everybody's Magazine,* October 1908.

Stokes, J. G. P. "Reasons for Supporting Debs" *Outlook,* XC (October 24, 1908).

Stone, Irving. *Adversary in the House* E. V. Debs . Garden City, New York, Doubleday and Co., 1947.

Swinton, John. "1860—Lincoln; Debs—1905," Terre Haute, Indiana, Viquesney Printing Co., 1905.

Superintendent's Reports 1869—1875, "Curriculum." Bound and stored in vault of Wiley High School, Terre Haute, Indiana.

Thomas, Norman. "Eugene V. Debs," *Current History,* December 1926.

Trachtenberg, Alexander. *The Heritage of Gene Debs,* New York, International Publishers, 1918.

Speeches of Eugene V. Debs. New York, International Publishers, 1928.

A WORD.

The pen of the author of this book has been forever silenced by death. To the suffering souls who vision life only within gray stone walls, through cold steel bars, whose days are sunless, whose nights are starless, from whose melancholy hearts hope has fled—to these, all of them victims of a cruel and inhuman social system, this volume is re-dedicated in tender and loving commemoration of the writer by his brother and fellow-worker.   THEODORE DEBS.

"The social environment is the cultural medium of criminality; the criminal is the microbe—an element that becomes important only when it finds a medium which will cause it to ferment. *Every society has the criminals it deserves"*.
                    —LASCUSSAGNE.

MY PRISON CREED.

While there is a lower class I am in it;
While there is a criminal element I am of it;
While there's a soul in prison I am not free.

BEYOND.

Beyond these walls,
  Sweet Freedom calls;
In accents clear and brave she speaks,
And lo! my spirit scales the peaks.

Beyond these bars,
  I see the stars;
God's glittering heralds beckon me—
My soul is winged: Behold, I'm free!

To the countless thousands of my brothers and sisters who have suffered the cruel and pitiless torture and degradation of imprisonment in the jails, penitentiaries and other barbarous and brutalizing penal institutions of capitalism under our much-vaunted Christian civilization, and who in consequence now bear the ineffaceable brand of convicts and criminals, this volume is dedicated with affection and devotion by one of their number.

ACKNOWLEDGMENT AND APPRECIATION

The deep, sincere and grateful acknowledgment due the many friends and comrades, near and far, not only in this country but beyond the seas, who followed me so faithfully through the very prison doors and who sympathized with all their loyal hearts and literally shared every hour of my imprisonment, can never be expressed in words. By day and by night these devoted comrades were with me, so near that I could feel the touch of their loving hands and hear their loyal heart-beats in my prison cell.

From all directions, by mail and by wire, there came the message of comfort and good cheer from men, women and children, thousands upon thousands of them, the number increasing with the passing days to attest the growing sympathy and loyalty of the host of steadfast devotees.

How lightly the sentence I was serving rested upon me with such a noble legion of loving comrades to cheer and sustain me every moment of my imprisonment! To them I owe a debt of love and gratitude that never can be paid. They all but entered the prison and served my sentence for me; they not only sent me their precious and heartening messages, food prepared with their own dear hands, wearing apparel, and other gifts as testimonials of their faith and constancy, but

they came in person over long and wearied
stretches of travel to give aid and comfort and
affectionate ministration in every way in their
power.

The tender regard, the loving care, the unfail-
ing devotion shown to my wife to relieve her
loneliness and to enable her to bear with fortitude
the trials of my prison days; the aid and assistance so freely and generously given to my
brother in meeting party demands and in the discharge of official duties in my absence, constitute
a chapter of loving service and self-consecration,
a manifestation of the utter divinity of human
comradeship that can not be traced upon the
written page but must remain forever a hallowed
memory.

To these dear friends and comrades, beloved
and appreciated beyond expression, I now make
grateful acknowledgement and give thanks with
all my heart. I can not here attempt to call them
all by name, but vividly do they appear before me
in their radiant and inspiring comradeship, and to
each and all of them do I give hail and greeting
and pledge my love, my gratitude and my unre-
laxing fidelity to the cause they so bravely sustained and vindicated during my prison days.

To these brave, noble hearts I owe my life and
liberation. But for their loyal devotion and un-
tiring agitation my life would have gone out behind prison walls.

And now in turn I sense the solemn duty to

51

ACKNOWLEDGMENT AND APPRECIATION

join and persist in the demand for the release of
all other comrades still immured in dungeon cells
until the last prisoner of the class war has secured
his liberation.

INTRODUCTION.

While still an inmate of the United States Penitentiary at Atlanta, Georgia, the suggestion was made to me by interested publishers that upon my release I write a series of articles describing my prison experience. The suggestion, coming from various sources, appealed to me for the reason that I saw in it an opportunity to give the general public certain information in regard to the prison, based upon my personal observation and experience, that I hoped might result in some beneficial changes in the management of prisons and in the treatment of their inmates.

While serving my term at Atlanta I saw so much that offended me, as being needlessly cruel and abusive; I came in direct contact with so many of the victims of prison mismanagement and its harsh and inhuman regulations, that I resolved upon my release to espouse the cause of these unfortunates and do what was in my power to put an end to the wrongs and abuses of which they were the victims under the present system.

If there are men and women anywhere among us who need to have their condition looked into in an enlightened, sympathetic and helpful way; if there are any whose very helplessness should excite our interest, to say nothing of our compassion as human beings, they are the inmates of our jails, prisons and penitentiaries, hidden from our view by grim walls, who suffer in silence, and whose cries are not permitted to reach our ears.

The inmates of prisons are not the irretrievably vicious and depraved element they are commonly believed to be, but upon the average they are like ourselves, and it is more often their misfortune than their crime that is responsible for their plight. If these prisoners were treated as they should be, with due regard to all the circumstances surrounding their cases, a very great majority of them, instead of being diseased, crazed and wrecked morally and physically under a cruel and degrading prison system, would be reclaimed and restored to society, the better, not the worse, for their experience.

In this, society as well as the individual would be the gainer, and to that extent crime in the community would cease.

Shortly after my release negotiations were concluded with the Bell Syndicate of New York for the publication of a series of prison articles to appear simultaneously in newspapers subscribing for them throughout the country. These articles, written for the capitalist-owned dailies, had to be prepared with a distinct reserve to insure their publication. This concession had to be made to avoid peremptory refusal of any hearing at all through the public press of the abuses and crimes which cried to heaven from behind prison walls.

It was therefore made a specific condition by the Syndicate and a guarantee to the papers subscribing for the articles that they should contain no "propaganda". The reason for this precaution on the part of the capitalist press is perfectly obvious and self-evident. Any intelligent understanding of the prison system as it now exists, based upon a true knowledge of the graft and corruption which prevail in its management, and of the appalling vice and immorality, cruelty and crime for which the prison is responsible and of which the inmates are the helpless victims, would inevitably mean the impeachment of our smug and self-complacent capitalist society at the bar of civilization, and the utter condemnation of the capitalist system of which the prison is a necessary adjunct, and of which these rich and powerful papers are the official organs and mouthpieces.

It was this that these papers had in mind when the assurance had to be given them that my articles would contain no "propaganda".

They did not want, nor do they now, the truth, the whole truth, and nothing but the truth, about our corrupt, brutalizing and criminal-breeding prison system to be known to the people, for they know not only that such a revelation would shock and scandalize the country but that it would expose and condemn the impoverishing, enslaving and crime-inciting social system of which they are the organs and beneficiaries.

When the opening article appeared the following bracketed notice was placed at its head:

("The views expressed in this article and in the others of this series are those of Eugene V. Debs and not of the Bell Syndicate, Inc. Mr. Debs has agreed not to insert any political propaganda into the article.")

Well does the capitalist press know that the naked truth about our foul prison system would be the deadliest kind of "political propaganda" against the capitalist system which created and is responsible for that festering evil, and against the equally foul political parties which uphold capitalism and perpetuate its corrupt and criminal misrule.

The capitalist dailies were desirous enough to have the articles, knowing they would create interest and have a wide reading, thus proving a feature of value to them, but they wanted them toned down, emasculated in fact, to render them harmless as possible and at the same time secure them against the danger they so mortally dread of containing other than their own "political propaganda". They insist upon a monopoly of their own brand, and such is their faith in its efficacy, that they will tolerate no encroachment upon their vested propaganda interests.

Soon after the first article appeared complaints were made from various quarters that there was "propaganda" in the series. This justified them in expunging entire paragraphs and finally in not publishing at all the closing articles of the series.

The first eight and the tenth to the thirteenth chapters in this book constitute the series of twelve articles given to the daily press through the Bell Syndicate and are here reprinted through their courtesy.

In this connection it should be said that but nine of the twelve articles furnished the press were published, and in some instances the papers struck out parts and paragraphs they did not like on the ground that they were "propaganda" or "too radical", thus withholding from their readers the very points of information and the very vital passages to which the writer was most anxious to give publicity for the end he had in view.

To the twelve original articles there have been added three chapters for the purpose not only of amplifying the treatment of the subject, but that the writer might discuss more critically and fundamentally the vital phases of the prison question, including especially the cause of and the responsibility for this crying evil, than was possible in the newspaper articles.

There has also been added an Address before the Nineteenth Century Club at Delmonico's,

New York City, on Prison Labor, Its Effects on Industry and Trade, March 21st., 1899; an article contributed to the Century Magazine for July, 1922, and another to The World Tomorrow for August, 1922, and reproduced here by the courtesy of those periodicals.

In the latter chapters I have undertaken to show that the prison in our modern life is essentially a capitalistic institution, an inherent and inseparable part of the social and economic system under which the mass of mankind are ruthlessly exploited and kept in an improverished state, as a result of which the struggle for existence, cruel and relentless at best, drives thousands of its victims into the commission of offenses which they are forced to expiate in the dungeons provided for them by their masters.

The prison as a rule, to which there are few execeptions, is for the poor.

The owning and ruling class hold the keys of the prison the same as they do of the mill and mine. They are the keepers of both and their exploited slaves are the inmates and victims of both.

As long as the people are satisfied with capitalism they will have to bear its consequences in the prison sentences imposed upon increasing numbers of them, and also bear the poverty and misery which fall to the lot of those who toil and produce the wealth of the nation.

The prison at present is at best a monumental

evil and a burning shame to society. It ought not merely to be reformed but abolished as an institution for the punishment and degradation of unfortunate human beings.

EUGENE V. DEBS.

Terre Haute, Indiana, July 1st., 1926.

CHAPTER I.

THE RELATION OF SOCIETY TO THE CONVICT.

A prison is a cross section of society in which every human strain is clearly revealed. An average prison, and its inmates, in point of character, intelligence and habits, will compare favorably with any similar number of persons outside of prison walls.

I believe that my enemies, as well as my friends, will concede to me the right to arrive at some conclusions with respect to prisons and prisoners by virtue of my personal experience, for I have been an inmate of three county jails, one state prison and one federal penitentiary. A total of almost four years of my life has been spent behind the bars as a common prisoner; but an experience of such a nature cannot be measured in point of years. It is measured by the capacity to see, to feel and to comprehend the social significance and the human import of the prison in its relation to society.

In the very beginning I desire to stress the point that I have no personal grievance to air as a result of my imprisonment. I was never personally mistreated, and no man was ever brutal to me. On the other hand, during my prison years I was treated uniformly with a peculiar personal kindliness by my fellow-prisoners, and not infrequently by officials. I do not mean to imply that any special favors were ever accorded me. I never requested nor would I accept anything that could not be obtained on the same basis by the humblest prisoner. I realized that I was a convict, and as such I chose to share the lot of those around me on the same rigorous terms that were imposed upon all.

It is true that I have taken an active part in public affairs for the past forty years. In a consecutive period of that length a man is bound to acquire a reputation of one kind or another. My adversaries and I are alike perfectly satisfied with the sort of reputation they have given me. A man should take to himself no discomfort from an opinion expressed or implied by his adversary, but it is difficult, and often-times humiliating to attempt to justify the kindness of one's friends. When my enemies do not indulge in calumny I find it exceedingly difficult to answer their charges against me. In fact, I am guilty of believing in a broader humanity and a nobler civilization. I am guilty also of being opposed to force and violence. I am guilty of believing that the human race can be humanized and enriched in every spiritual inference through the saner and more beneficent processes of peaceful persuasion applied to material problems rather than through wars, riots and bloodshed. I went to prison because I was guilty of believing

these things. I have dedicated my life to these beliefs and shall continue to embrace them to the end.

My first prison experience occurred in 1894 when, as president of the American Railway Union I was locked up in the Cook County Jail, Chicago, because of my activities in the great railroad strike that was in full force at that time. I was given a cell occupied by five other men. It was infested with vermin, and sewer rats scurried back and forth over the floors of that human cesspool in such numbers that it was almost impossible for me to place my feet on the stone floor. Those rats were nearly as big as cats, and vicious. I recall a deputy jailer passing one day with a fox-terrier. I asked him to please leave his dog in my cell for a little while so that the rat population might thereby be reduced. He agreed, and the dog was locked up with us, but not for long, for when two or three sewer rats appeared the terrier let out such an appealing howl that the jailer came and saved him from being devoured.

I recall seeing my fellow inmates of Cook County Jail stripping themselves to their waists to scratch the bites inflicted by all manner of nameless vermin, and when they were through the blood would trickle down their bare bodies in tiny red rivulets. Such was the torture suffered by these men who as yet had been convicted of no crime, but who were awaiting trial. I was given

a cell that a guard took the pains to tell me had
been occupied by Prendergast, who assassinated
Mayor Carter H. Harrison. He showed me the
bloody rope with which Prendergast had been
hanged and intimated with apparent glee spark-
ling in his eyes that the same fate awaited me.
His intimation was perhaps predicated upon what
he read in the newspapers of that period, for my
associates and I were accused of every conceivable crime in connection with that historic strike.
I was shown the cells that had been occupied by
the Chicago anarchists who were hanged, and was
told that the gallows awaited the man in this
country who strove to better the living conditions
of his fellowmen.

Such was my introduction to prison life. I
can never forget the sobbing and screaming that
I heard, while in Cook County Jail, from the
fifty or more women prisoners who were there.
From that moment I felt my kinship with every
human being in prison, and I made a solemn resolution with myself that if ever the time came
and I could be of any assistance to those unfortunate souls, I would embrace the opportunity
with every ounce of my strength. I felt myself
on the same human level with those Chicago
prisoners. I was not one whit better than they.
I felt that they had done the best they could with
their physical and mental equipment to improve
their sad lot in life, just as I had employed my
physical and mental equipment in the service

of those about me, to whom I was responsible, whose lot I shared,—and the energy expended had landed us both in jail. There we were on a level with each other.

With my associate officers of the American Railway Union I was transferred to the McHenry County Jail, Woodstock, Illinois, where I served a six months' sentence in 1895 for contempt of court in connection with the federal proceedings that grew out of the Pullman strike in 1894. My associates served three months, but my time was doubled because the federal judges considered me a dangerous man and a menace to society. In the years that intervened some national attention was paid to me because I happened to have been named a presidential candidate in several successive campaigns.

But there was no real rejoicing from the influential and powerful side of our national life until June, 1918, when I was arrested by Department of Justice agents in Cleveland for a speech that I had delivered in Canton, Ohio. I was taken to the Cuyahoga County Jail, and when the inmates heard that I was in prison with them there was a mild to-do about it, and they congratulated me through their cells. A deputy observed the fraternity that had sprung up, and I was removed to a more remote corner. Just after I retired that Sunday midnight I heard a voice calling my name through a small aperture and inquiring if I were asleep. I replied no.

"Well, you've been nominated for Congress from the Fifth District in Indiana. Good luck to you!" he said.

When a jury in the federal court in Cleveland found me guilty of violating the Espionage Law, through a speech delivered in Canton on June 16, 1918, Judge Westenhaver sentenced me to serve ten years in the West Virginia State Penitentiary, at Moundsville. This prison had entered into an agreement with the government to receive and hold federal prisoners for the sum of forty cents per day per prisoner. On June 2, 1919, the State Board of Control wrote a letter to the Federal Superintendent of Prisons complaining that my presence had cost the state $500 a month for extra guards and requested that the government send more federal prisoners to Moundsville to meet this expense. The government could not see its way clear to do this, since it was claimed there was plenty of room at Atlanta, and if, as the State Board of Control averred, I was a liability rather than an asset to the State, the government would transfer me to its own federal prison at Atlanta, which it did on June 13, 1919, exactly two months after the date on which I began to serve my ten years imprisonment—a sentence which was commuted by President Warren G. Harding on Christmas day, 1922.

I was aware of a marvelous change that came over me during and immediately after my first incarceration. Before that time I had looked upon prisons and prisoners as a rather sad affair, but a condition that somehow could not be remedied. It was not until I was a prisoner myself that I realized, and fully comprehended, the prison problem and the responsibility that, in the last analysis, falls directly upon society itself.

The prison problem is directly co-related with poverty, and poverty as we see it today is essentially a social disease. It is a cancerous growth in a vulnerable spot of the social system. There should be no poverty among hard-working people. Those who produce should have, but we know that those who produce the most—that is, those who work hardest, and at the most difficult and most menial tasks, have the least. But of this I shall have more to say. After all, the purpose of these chapters is to set forth the prison problem as one of the most vital concerns of present day society. A prison is an institution to which any of us may go at any time. Some of us go to prison for breaking the law, and some of us for upholding and abiding by the Constitution to which the law is supposed to adhere. Some go to prison for killing their fellowmen, and others for believing that murder is a violation of one of the Commandments. Some go to prison for stealing, and others for believing that a better system can be provided and maintained than one that makes it necessary for a man to steal in order to live.

67

The prison has always been a part of human society. It has always been deemed an essential factor in organized society. The prison has its place and its purpose in every civilized nation. It is only in uncivilized places that you will not find the prison. Man is the only animal that constructs a cage for his neighbor and puts him in it. To punish by imprisonment, involving torture in every conceivable form, is a most tragic phase in the annals of mankind. The ancient idea was that the more cruel the punishment the more certain the reformation. This idea, fortunately, has to a great extent receded into the limbo of savagery whence it sprang. We now know that brutality begets brutality, and we know that through the centuries there has been a steady modification of discipline and method in the treatment of prisoners. I will concede that the prison today is not nearly as barbarous as it was in the past, but there is yet room for vast improvement, and it is for the purpose of causing to be corrected some of the crying evils that obtain in present day prisons and making possible such changes in our penal system as will mitigate the unnecessary suffering of the helpless and unfortunate inmates that I set myself the task of writing these articles before I turn my attention to anything else.

It has been demonstrated beyond cavil that the more favorable prison conditions are to the inmates, the better is the result for society. We should bear in mind that few men go to prison for life, and the force that swept them into prison sweeps them out again, and they must go back into the social stream and fight for a living. I have heard people refer to the "criminal countenance". I never saw one. Any man or woman looks like a criminal behind bars. Criminality is often a state of mind created by circumstances or conditions which a person has no power to control or direct; he may be swamped by overwhelming influences that promise but one avenue to peace of mind; in sheer desperation the distressed victim may choose the one way, only to find he has broken the law—and at the end of the tape loom the turrets of the prison. Once a convict always a convict. That is one brand that is never outworn by time.

How many people in your community would be out of prison if they would frankly confess their sins against society and the law were enforced against them?

How many lash and accuse themselves of nameless and unnumbered crimes for which there is no punishment save the torment visited upon the individual conscience? Yet, they who so accuse themselves, assuming there exist reasons to warrant accusation, would never admit to themselves the possession of a criminal countenance. In Atlanta Prison I made it a point to seek out those men that were called "bad". I found the men, but I did not find them bad. They responded to kindness with the simplicity of a child. In no other institution on the face of the earth are men so sensitive as those who are caged in prison. They are ofttimes terror-stricken; they do not see the years ahead which may be full of promise, they see only the walls and the steel bars that separate them from their loved ones. I never saw those bars nor the walls in the nearly three years that I spent in Atlanta. I was never conscious of being a prisoner. If I had had that consciousness it would have been tantamount to an admission of guilt, which I never attached to myself.

It was because I was oblivious of the prison as a thing that held my body under restraint that I was able to let my spirit soar and commune with the friends of freedom everywhere. The intrinsic me was never in prison. No matter what might have happened to me I would still have been at large in the spirit. Many years ago, when I made my choice of what life had to offer, I realized, saw plainly, that the route I had chosen would be shadowed somewhere by the steel bars of a prison gate. I accepted it, and understood it perfectly. I consider that the years I spent in prison were necessary to complete my particular education for the part that I am permitted to play in human affairs. I would certainly not exchange that experience, if I could, to be President of the United States, although some people indulge the erroneous belief that I have coveted that office in several political campaigns.

The time will come when the prison as we now know it will disappear, and the hospital and asylums and farm will take its place. In that day we shall have succeeded in taking the jail out of man as well as taking man out of jail.

Think of sending a man out from prison and into the world with a shoddy suit of clothes that is recognized by every detective as a prison garment, a pair of paper shoes, a hat that will shrink to half its size when it rains, a railroad ticket, a five dollar bill and seven cents carfare! Bear in mind that the railroad ticket does not necessarily take a man back into the bosom of his family, but to the place where he was convicted of crime. In other words a prisoner, after he has served his sentence, goes back to the scene of his crime. Society's responsibility ends there —so it thinks. But does it? I say not. With the prison system what it is, with my knowledge of what it does to men after they get into prison, and with the contempt with which society regards them after they come out, the wonder is not that we have periodical crime waves in times of economic and industrial depression, but the wonder is that the social system is not constantly in convulsions as a result of the desperate deeds of the thousands of men and women who pour in and pour out of our jails and prisons in never ending streams of human misery and suffering.

But society has managed to protect itself against the revenge of the prisoner by dehumanizing him while he is in prison. The process is slow, by degrees, like polluted water trickling from the slimy mouth of a corroded and encrusted spout—but it is a sure process. When a man has remained in prison over a certain length of time his spirit is doomed. He is stripped of his manhood. He is fearful and afraid. He has not been redeemed. He has been crucified. He has not reformed. He has become a roving animal casting about for prey, and too weak to seize it. He is often too weak to live even by the law of the fang and the claw. He is not acceptable even in the jungle of human life, for the denizens of the wilderness demand strength and bravery as the price and tax of admission.

Withal, a prison is a most optimistic institution. Every man somehow believes that he can "beat" his sentence. He relies always upon the "technical point" which he thinks has been overlooked by his lawyers. He sometimes imagines that fond friends are busily working in his behalf on the outside. But in a little while the bubble breaks, disillusion appears, the letters from home become fewer and fewer, and the prisoner in tears of desperation resigns himself to his lot. Society has won in him an abiding enemy. If, perchance, he is not wholly broken by the wrecking process by the time his sentence is served, he may seek to strike back. In either case society has lost.

I do not know how many prisoners came to me with their letters soaked in tears. They sought my advice. They believed I could help them over the rough edges. I could do nothing but listen and offer them my kindness and counsel. They would stop me in the corridors, and on my way to the mess room and say: "Mr. Debs, I want to get a minute with you to tell you about my case". Or, "Mr. Debs, will you read this letter from my wife; she says she can't stand the gaff any longer". Or, "Mr. Debs, my daughter has gone on the town; what in God's name can you do about it?" What could I do about it? I could only pray with all my heart for strength to contribute toward the re-arrangement of human affairs so that this needless suffering might be abolished. Two or three concrete cases will suffice as examples of the suffering that I saw.

Jenkins, but that is not his name, was a railroad man. Aged, 35. Married and six children; the oldest a daughter, aged 16 years. His wages were too small to support his family in decency. He broke into a freight car in interstate commerce. Sentenced to five years in Atlanta. He received a letter a little while before his term expired telling him that his daughter had been seduced and was in the "red light" district. This man came to me with his tears and swore he would spend the rest of his life tracking down

---

73

the man who ruined his daughter, and, upon finding him, he would kill him. For days I sought that man out and talked with him, and persuaded him against his rash program. His wife stopped writing to him. She had found an easier, but a sadder, way of solving her economic problems. His home was completely broken up by the time he got out of prison.

Another prisoner who had been a small trades-man, married and the father of eight children, also broke into a freight car. It was his first offence. He got five years. He showed me a letter from his wife saying there was no food in the house and no shoes for the children. The landlord had threatened them with eviction. That man was thirsting for revenge. Society had robbed his family of the breadwinner. The mother had too many children to leave them and work herself. If society deprives a family of their provider should it not provide for the family? It would have been more humane to have sent the whole family to prison.

Another young man, aged 25, showed me a letter from his wife. He was married a little while before he was convicted. His wife was pregnant and was living with the prisoner's invalid mother. She had written to him saying that unless she got relief from somewhere both herself and his mother had made up their minds to commit sui-cide. They were destitute. They had been refused further credit. They could endure the misery no longer.

Many men attempt suicide in prison. One of the most damaging influences in prison life is the long sentence. It produces a reaction in the heart and mind of the man who receives it that defeats its intended purpose.

Every prison of which I have any acknowledge is a breeding place for evil, an incubator for crime. This is especially true about the influence of the prison upon the youth and young man. Of him I shall write in my next article.

CHAPTER II.

THE PRISON AS AN INCUBATOR OF CRIME.

The boy who is arrested for the first time charged with an offence against the law, constitutes one of the most vital and portentous phases of the prison problem. He may be entirely innocent, but this does not save him from going to jail and have a jail record fastened upon him as an unending stigma.

If he happens to be a poor boy, as is most frequently the case, he may be kept in jail, and often is, for an indefinite period, notwithstanding the constitutional guarantees of a speedy trial. Very often this delay occurs through the manipulation of the sheriff who derives a revenue from feeding prisoners and keeping them in the county jail. Thus, the sheriff's income is enlarged. It is a notorious fact that prisoners by hundreds all over the country are kept in jails, and their trials are delayed or postponed because the sheriff and others derive a direct income thereby under a contract with the county for feeding prisoners.

The scandalous effects of this pernicious arrangement are apparent in the miserable food given to prisoners in the average county jail; helpless and untried boys and young men, possibly innocent, are kept in jail to their physical and moral undoing.

Just here it may be pertinent to observe that the average county jail is an absolutely unfit place in which to lodge any human being, however low his social status may be. As these lines are written, this charge is confirmed in the report of a state commission condemning the jails of Indiana as unsanitary, foul and disease-breeding, wholly unfit for human occupation. But if every state in the union were to appoint a commission to investigate its jails and prisons the conclusion would be the same as that reached by the Indiana body.

We must bear in mind that the boy or young man who is put in the toils is usually poor, and his friends are without any considerable influence in the community. It may be that his parents have had to devote every minute of their time to the proposition of making an uncertain living; the boy and his brothers and sisters, if he has any, are neglected; they do not receive the proper attention in the home that is the right of every growing child. Their education is often neglected for the sufficient reason that their labor power, such as it is, is required to help maintain what passes for a home, but which is often a shack, a lair, a place in which mother and father and their brood come to lay their tired and weary bodies after the day's work is done. Such an atmosphere is not conducive to the sweeter amenities of life, but begets a sad, sordid and drab existence, out of which all hope, some day, to climb.

If the boy be a spirited lad he will rebel against the conditions that obtain at home, the significance of which he does not in the least perceive. If, in this trying period of his young manhood, he had at least someone who would extend the helping hand, speak the kindly word, and give the encouraging embrace, the boy might respond to these beneficent influences and direct his steps into avenues of useful citizenship. But up to this moment society has not been collectively interested in alleviating the conditions that make for the so-called criminal. Society does appear to be highly indignant when the boy or young man rebels and strikes back in the only way that he knows how to strike—in the way that he has been taught by the social conditions in which he lives. The policeman, the sheriff and the judge do possess intelligence enough to see the fact, but what they do not see is the impulse in the boy to live, which is before the fact, and the consequence of their own blindness which comes in due time after the fact.

I do not know if I should go to the length of saying with the poet that "no hell is so black as the court that sentences man to it", but I have no hesitancy in declaring that no social system is so stupid as the one that sows the seeds of vice and crime and later becomes purple with indignation and horror when the crop is ripe for picking.

As ye sow, so shall ye reap!

It may be unfortunate and a bit disconcerting that the inexorable law of compensation must forever operate in the affairs of society, for if it could be repealed, or even suspended for a time, mankind might be spared the unpleasantness of gazing upon some of the human manifestations that are wrought, willy-nilly, against the intentions of most of us, who have, I take it, a more or less generous regard for our fellow man.

Holding men in jail week after week, month after month, as is commonly the case, is not only one of the inexcusable vices of the present system of administering the law, but is directly responsible for debauching the manhood of the victims especially the young and those of maturer age who have committed their first offence.

If, finally, upon trial, persons so held are found to be innocent of the charges against them, or if the cases are dismissed for want of evidence upon which to convict them, or other reasons, an irreparable injury has been done them by society, not only in point of moral contamination, but in branding them as jail birds, the record of which is ineffaceable and might as well be stamped upon their foreheads. That record will follow them through every avenue and lane of life and will serve to convict them in advance of any charge that any malevolent person might subsequently bring against them.

The most vicious phase of all in this connection is the fact that if the victim is finally convicted after lying and festering in jail for three months, six months, or even a year or more, the time thus served is not allowed to count in his prison sentence, which has to be served in full in addition to the time spent in the county jail.

In the light of these flagrant abuses of our helpless fellow beings, what else can the prison be considered than a breeder of vice, immorality and disease, and condemned as an incubator for crime?

Think of a boy 13, or 14 years of age, perhaps wrongly accused, in such a place; among the confirmed and hardened criminals of all types, learning their language, and absorbing their moral perversions, and witnessing their spiritual decay!

How does such a boy feel, and what must be his reaction to such a rude shock to his young life! I am sure I know, for I have been with him. I have seen his fear-stricken countenance, felt his trembling hand in mine, and heard his troubled heart-beat.

Society, and those who function for it in the name of the law should pause long and consider well before putting the boy in jail for the first time,—especially the boy who has not the few dollars that are sometimes necessary to keep him out of jail. That boy may, by such initiation into the ways of law and justice, be started upon a career of reprisal for which society may pay dearly, perhaps with life itself in the end.

Every community should have at least as much interest in the condition and management of its jail as it pretends to have in its schoolhouse, and as it certainly has in its center of amusement and entertainment.

The jail, after all, indifferent or scornful as we may be to the fact, is not only an integral part of the social fabric, but is a darkened room separated only by a shallow door from the rest of the apartments in the community house. If pestilence prevails there, if moral miasma issues forth from that cesspool the community is to just that extent contaminated and imperilled.

The abuses of the prison system, and the crimes against criminals in the perverted name of law and order, are as constantly visited upon the community responsible for them as a devastating plague follows in the wake of disease and death-dealing germs.

Every community should look into its jail, find out who is there and why, how the prisoners are fed, and if they are held for purposes of graft that finds its way into the pockets of the petty politicians, the chief of whom in this case is the sheriff of the county. The community should insist that the men held in its jail be either tried or released, for every hour that a man is held in jail he is a liability, not an asset, to the community which pays the tax that is levied against it to

feed and shelter its erring members. From the
purely selfish, monetary standpoint, if not from
the broader social questions raised, society at
large, and each component part of society, should
be concerned in this problem.

From the standpoint of the erring boy, the
young man, and the first offender the prison
problem is not the last rung of the social ladder
that he must mount, but the first one. Shall he
be branded with the flaming torch that writes in
scarlet letters the word "Convict" across his
brow, and condemned to a fugitive existence for
the remainder of his days because he chanced to
be unfortunate either through the manner of
birth, or through circumstances that he could not
control, or because of direful conditions with
which he could not cope with his poor physicial
or material equipment? For good or for bad, is
he not an inevitable product of the social system?
And should he be doomed at the first crossroad
in his young life because society had failed to
prepare for him a kindlier reception at his birth,
and ignored him thereafter, except as it might
exploit whatever brawn or cunning that he possessed.

Youthful and first offenders are also the legitimate prey of unscrupulous lawyers, the hangers-
on of police courts, who seek to extract every dollar the accused can beg or borrow, and who all
the while know that the track is clear between his
so-called client and the penitentiary. Time with-

out number this type of lawyer keeps the prisoner in a county jail under the pretext given to the court that he is not ready for trial, that there is more evidence to be obtained for his client, when as a matter of fact the mercenary lawyer in his craven heart knows he is seeking, not for evidence with which to liberate the defenceless victim but to extract the last possible penny from the man in jail before he is railroaded beyond his reach to the penitentiary. I have known of helpless prisoners to be pursued by avaricous lawyers after they had begun to serve their sentences, and the simple-hearted victims would often write to their destitute families asking them to send their last dollars to attorneys in exchange for a gilded lie which the simple prisoners made themselves believe was a fresh promise of liberty.

Let us now deal with the first offender who, after interminable delays, is convicted and his money gone. He has been pilloried, put on exhibition in the courtroom before the gaze of the curious, his plight ridiculed in the press. He feels himself an outcast, friendless, and indeed he is. The judge pronounces the victim's doom from an elevated throne and passes on to the next case. Persons accused of crime lose their identity as human beings and become "cases", just as workingmen are only "hands" to some employers. The sentence of the law is executed with all the solemnity and ceremony of a funeral, and the culprit, with head bowed either from grief or rage, is led from the courtroom between two feelingless factotums to begin his punishmen—justice is served, society is avenged, and all is well once more. But is it? Not so fast!

The victim has already suffered every torment and feels the keenest sense of shame and humiliation, but this does not count in the matter of atonement. He goes back to jail until the sheriff can arrange to take him to the "pen".

The fateful day arrives! He is manacled, sometimes hand and foot, and put on a train where everyone learns he is a convict and secretly mocks him.

He is delivered, signed for, sheds his name and receives a number. He is no longer a man but a thing. He has ceased to be a human being. He is stripped naked under the clubs of guards who hurl insults and epithets at him about his body. He is put into a cheap prison garb that in itself proclaims the status to which he has been reduced. He is examined in a rude and perfunctory way by the physician's assistant who himself may be a convict. He is made to sign a document stating where his body is to be shipped in case of death. He is handled as if he were a bag of malt as he goes through the Bertillon system. Note is taken and a record made of every mark upon his body. All his personal effects are taken from him. These are supposed to be shipped back to his home, if he has one, and if he has money to pay the charges. The chances are, however, his

84

effects will be stolen before they leave the prison, if they have any value.

In this particular I have had some personal experience, for when I went to Atlanta Prison only a part of my effects that should have been sent to my home arrived there. Whereas I indicated that the traveling bag that I carried there with me should be left among my personal possessions in the prison, I was given a cardboard tomato case when I left as travelling equipment. Among other things, I especially recall that cuff and shirt buttons, small trinkets that were given to me as mementoes by friends, and some shirts and other articles that were sent to me, were stolen after I arrived in Atlanta. I am making no charges, but stating a fact. What happened in my case happens in all cases in greater or smaller degree.

But as to the boy! The letter a week he is permitted to write is censored, and those he receives are opened and read. Little tokens of sentiment are extracted and thrown away. Even a lock of his mother's hair may not reach him.

If he should deign to go to the chapel to pray and take communion with his soul a guard sits over him with a club to sweeten his spirit and temper his piety.

The miserable food he receives starves, rather than feeds his body. The process in the mess room is more like slopping hogs than feeding humans, with the difference that hogs fatten

85

while humans starve. Here is where he makes his first acquaintance with stale old beef hearts and livers, and the classic brand of hash known in prison parlance as "concrete balls". The gravy is loud enough to talk and the oleo strong enough to walk. Bugs and worms figure proverbially in the prison menu.

The youth is beginning to realize the deadening monotony of prison life. His spirit is crushed. His sensibilities have become numb. His eyes do not see beyond the height of the gray prison walls upon which armed guards idle away the hours by watching eagerly for an opportunity to "wing" a fleeing jailbird.

He is put to work under the domination of the man with the club. He is watched and reported by the stool-pigeon who is himself a convict who has wormed into the graces of the officials and guards by spying upon his fellow prisoners. Every prison is a whispering gallery. Whatever is said is sure to reach the office promptly. No criticism is tolerated, and no complaint may get beyond the walls.

A prisoner cannot know the time of day, for there are no clocks in prison, the purpose being to cut the convict off as completely as possible from the outside world in which he had his being. The youth is thrown among all sorts and conditions of old and hardened convicts, and he soon acquires a new vocabulary peculiar to prison life. The foulest language flowers in the poisoned atmosphere of the prison pen. There he is schooled in the science of burglary taught by old professors in the art, and he learns at first hand from professional adepts all about every form of vice and crime known to man.

Here, also, where his sex instincts are suppressed, he is schooled in nameless forms of perversion of body, mind and soul that cause human beings to sink to abyssmal depths of depravity which the lower animals do not know. These perversions wreck the lives of countless thousands and send their wretched victims to premature and dishonored graves.

This is but one of the horrors of our modern civilization and the prison is its native breeding ground.

CHAPTER III.

I Become U. S. Convict No. 9653.

Warden Joseph Z. Terrell, of the West Virginia State Penitentiary at Moundsville, a former railroad station agent, had but recently been put in charge of the prison when I began to serve my ten-year sentence there on April 13, 1919. He treated me with perfect fairness, and I got along quite well and without the slightest trouble during the time I was in prison there.

On June 13, just two months after my sentence commenced, Mr. Terrell reluctantly informed me that I had been ordered transferred to Atlanta. The order came just in time to enable me to pack my belongings and get ready for the train that was to carry me to my southern destination.

Strict secrecy was enjoined by the government as to my removal, and especially as to the train upon which I was to take my departure. I have since been informed that before I left Moundsville the government officials commanded the two telegraph offices in Wheeling to accept no messages from reporters or other persons about my leaving West Virginia prison until the next morning. In spite of this attempt to effect profound secrecy as to my movements, a leak occurred somehow, for I was interviewed by a reporter

FEDERAL PRISON AT MOUNDSVILLE, W. VA., WHERE DEBS BEGAN HIS TEN-YEAR SEN-
TENCE ON APRIL 13, 1919.

89

the same day at Cincinnati en route to the south.

It appears that I was too near the coal fields in West Virginia, in which I had previously spent considerable time organizing the miners who were greatly agitated over my imprisonment. At one mass meeting at Charleston, which was attended by several thousand miners and other citizens, resolutions were passed threatening a march on Moundsville if I was not released.

Warden Terrell gave me a friendly introduction to U. S. Marshal Smith, who with his three deputies, took me in charge on arrival at Wheeling, whither the warden and his son had taken me in their automobile. The marshal and his deputies treated me with all consideration over the entire journey. The marshal bore a letter from Warden Terrell to Warden Fred. G. Zerbst at Atlanta, commending me on the basis of my prison record.

Shortly after the noon hour on the following day, June 14, we arrived in Atlanta. The marshal called for a taxicab.

"Where do you want to go?" asked the chauffeur.

"Take us to your best penitentiary," replied the marshal. Less than half an hour later we were landed at the gates of my new home, and I was delivered, signed for, and the marshal and his deputies took their departure, wishing me a pleasant stay.

In the massive main corrior in which I found

myself I had my first view and received my first
impression of the sinister institution, known as
the U. S. Penitentiary at Atlanta. It seemed to
me like a vast sepulchre in which the living dead
had been sequestered by society. Through the
steel gate at the end of the corridor I could see
human forms hurrying back and forth under the
watchful eyes of guards with clubs, and they appeared to me with all the uncanniness of spectral
shapes in the infernal regions. I was perfectly
calm and self-possessed for I had made up my
mind from the beginning that whatever my prison
experience might be I should face it without fear
or regret.

Such serenity is always vouchsafed by the
psychology of the man who follows the dictates of
his own conscience and is true to his own soul.
I could not help feeling aware of the curiosity
which my presence aroused among the convicts
and some of the officials. A few of the latter, I
observed, smothered whatever interest, hostile or
kindly, they may have felt over my presence by
a Sphinx-like sullenness which I readily comprehended.

There seems to be a studied mental attitude
on the part of most prison officials I have met,
particularly the guards, that has for its purpose
to impress upon the prisoner that the official is
wholly disinterested in the human equation, in the
natural impulses that make us what we are. He
strives to appear as unhuman as possible, and

this psychological sub-normality on his part comes to fruitage in what is often his inhuman conduct toward the prisoner. So far as the prisoners were concerned, I felt their kindly interest expressed in their furtive glances toward me, and their good will was apparent on every hand.

The guard in charge conducted me to a shower bath where I divested myself of my clothing. Every article, including a quill toothpick, was taken from me and my garments were minutely searched. The guard, I wish to admit, treated me quite decently, although I confess that but for my having steeled myself against whatever might be in the program I should have felt outraged by the harsh and unfeeling method with which the thing was done.

The introduction a prisoner receives and the way be is put through the initial stages of his sentence are not calculated to impress him with the fact that a prison is a human institution. The rigorous treatment he receives will not convince him that he had been placed there to redeem him from his transgressions and reclaim him as a human being. On the contrary, the process embitters him against all who had any part in his plight, estranges him from whatever kindly influences that may still be operating in his behalf, and alienates him from society which, in the first and final analysis, is responsible for him, and, perhaps in the end must answer to him.

After the bath I was clothed in cheap faded

blue denim which had been discarded by some prisoner who had gone out into the world. In company with several others who, also, had just arrived, I was escorted to the kitchen where our first meal was served, the dinner hour in the general mess having passed. Save for the bread, I could not say what the meal consisted of as I could not make it out, nor did I attempt any internal analysis of the menu. The food and the manner in which it was served created nausea rather than an appetite. While we sat at the table a bulky guard stood over us swinging his club and delivering himself in a gruff voice of certain instructions as to table conduct at the prison. I suspected that a passage or two in his culinary flight was made for my benefit, and I applauded in silence.

A little later the routine led to the hospital, where I was subjected to a physical examination; sundry blanks and reports, descriptive of me and my physical condition, were filled out for the prison archives.

The "mugging gallery" was next visited and there two pictures were taken by a convict photographer—one profile and one full-face—for the rogue's gallery. Before the camera was snapped a narrow plate showing my registration number was put around my neck. I was next assigned to a temporary cell with one other convict who had arrived on the same train with me. He was a young man who had but recently married. He would serve a year for taking some goods out of a freight car to piece out his wages which were too small to provide for his family. I had been shocked when I first saw this young man on the train, his feet and hands shackled and an expression of mingled terror and humiliation upon his countenance. The sad picture of that wretched and dejected youth will forever remain in my memory. He was assigned to a sewing machine and he seemed happy when he could renew the missing buttons on my prison suit.

I was taken in turn to the office of the Protestant and Catholic chaplains who questioned me about my spiritual beliefs and denominational affiliation. I gladly affirmed the first in a way that I fear was not clearly comprehended by these estimable gentlemen of the cloth, whose intentions, I am sure, were the best; as regards the second inquiry, I had to disappoint both of my interrogators for in my mind true and sincere spirituality carries with it no theological or denominational partisanship.

On this point I should like to digress a moment to say that when I went to Atlanta prison attendance at the chapel services was compulsory. Guards with clubs in their hands and scowls on their faces were stationed inside of this sanctuary where pious appeals were made to the prisoners to emulate Jesus and follow His teachings. The setting and the appeal were most incongruous to say the least, and my refusal to attend such a ghastly travesty upon religious worship was later followed by an order that made chapel attendance optional with the prisoners. But the guards with clubs were not displaced and for that reason, if for no other, I did not attend.

The day following the inquisition in the office of the chaplains a number of us new arrivals—a dozen in all—black and white, stood around the desk of the deputy warden. It was a motley crew rather than a picturesque audience. I was in the midst of what are called the lowest types of criminals flanked by Negro murderers, and yet, I never felt myself more perfectly at one with my fellow beings. We were all on a dead level there and I felt my heart beat in unison with the heartbeats of those brothers of mine whose hunted looks and wretched appearance were proof enough to me that they had been denied a decent chance in the outer world; I felt that I, who had fared so infinitely better, was bound to love and serve them as best I could within the prison walls in which we were alike victims.

One of the Negroes in that little coterie said to another of his race a few days later in referring to me:

"I would stay here for life to see that man go out." He meant it. There was to me a whole beautiful Christly sermon in those few words for that poor unlettered black brother.

Seated at his desk the deputy warden delivered an odd admixture of instructions, orders and warnings. It was his official duty to relieve himself of the same homily on arrival of all incoming prisoners. We were given to understand that "the goblins would get us if we didn't watch out."

The deputy, who was a rigid orthodox Calvinist, had previously officiated as foreman of a chain gang in Fulton County, Georgia. In the lecture which he delivered to us he bore especially on the penalty that would be imposed for the use of foul language. He repeated some of the frightful words in common use in the vocabulary of convicts, and he threatened dire punishment to any who might repeat them. It is a fact, however, notwithstanding his rigorous discipline and his solemn threats and warnings, that foul language continued to flow. Its usage is fostered, not repressed, by club rule and black-hole torture.

I would be laying no flattering unction upon myself if I should say that merely by speaking kindly with my fellow prisoners, treating them as equals, making them feel as I felt that their interest was mine and mine was theirs, the use of foul language declined to such a happy degree in the prison that it was a matter of comment among the prisoners and officials. I remember especially one convict who had been in Atlanta many years and was destined to spend his remaining ones within those gray walls. This man had been cruelly treated all his life by guards.

He had known no law that was not enforced with the club. He had been brutalized, and whatever human impulses to do good he might have felt were crushed by those who held him captive.

This man used foul language the same as the rest. I understood the reason for it, and my sympathy went out to him. I put my arm across his shoulder and told him that if he must use that kind of language to please not employ it in my presence, not because it hurt me, I said, but because it hurt him.

"I hate to think of you," I said to him, "using that fine body of yours as a sewer from which to emit such filthy words." He perceived me, and soon this man's vocabulary was free from foulness except when he saw a stool-pigeon whom he loathed and abominated.

The deputy warden, upon hearing that this man had almost cleansed his vocabulary, sent for him one day and asked him how he had succeeded in doing it

"Mister Debs jest asked me to," he replied simply. "He is the only Christ I know anything about, 'cause I see how he lives and feels about these things. There is as much difference between Mister Debs and the rest of the people in this place as there is between mud and ice-cream." I know that my black brother greatly exaggerated my little part in his partial reformation. The good was in him, and I had merely brought it to his attention.

On leaving the deputy warden's office my fellow prisoners and I were returned to our temporary cells, and the following day we were assigned to our respective duties. I was given a clerical position in the clothing room where the outfiitting of the prisoners takes place, and where, also, prison supplies are stored and furnished to the several departments.

My duties were very simple and entirely agreeable as prison service. The official in charge treated me well and all the prisoners employed in that department vied with each other in helping me to get along. After the day's work we were allowed half an hour for exercise in the stockade before supper, for which twenty minutes was allowed. I was not eager about mealtime. I was in Atlanta prison nearly two weeks and pretty well starved before nature forced me to become receptive to the food and the manner in which it was served.

After a few days in a temporary cell I was assigned to my regular cage which was occupied by five other men, one of whom was a German, one a Jew, one an Irishman and two Americans. Being the latest arrival I should have occupied an upper bunk, but the German, who had the lower, insisted on taking the upper and giving me his own sleeping slab. He also insisted on making my bed, as I had some difficulty in making it up so it would pass inspection. He continued this kindness all the time I occupied that cell.

He likewise did my laundering of the smaller items of apparel that had to be done in our cells.

This German was sentenced for five years because some liquor had been found in the lodging house of which he was the proprietor and at which soldiers were quartered during the war. This is one of the many savage sentences that was brought to my personal attention, and which excited my indignation and revolt. I never knew a finer man, and I could not have been treated more kindly and considerately had these five convicts been my own brothers. Upon the German's release from prison be sent me a beautiful pipe, and he has been writing to me ever since.

Incidents of human kindness in this prison also could be multiplied by the hundreds. I would not give the impression that I was the sole beneficiary of these loving acts, for I have seen prisoners manifest the same regard toward each other, in spite of the harsh rules and regulations that seem to be calculated to crush magnanimity wherever it lifts its benevolent hand.

Just beyond the prison cells lies the campus along the walls of which guards in uniform pass back and forth swinging their Winchester rifles as if they were going out to shoot squirrels. The sight shocked me through and through with its horrid significance as a symbol of man's inhumanity under the prison regime. For paltry pay these guards contract to send a bullet through the heart of some hapless wretch who might have dreamed of liberty, and attempted to escape the tortures of a prison hell.

I had been in prison about a week when I first met Warden Zerbst, who sent for me and whom I met in his private office. He received me kindly and referred to the letter regarding me which he received from Warden Terrell at Moundsville. We had a frank conversation about the prison and my relation to it as an inmate.

I told Mr. Zerbst that the prison as an institution and I were deadly enemies, but that within the walls I should observe the rules and get along without trouble. I gave him to understand that I neither desired, expected, nor would I accept any privileges or favors that were denied to other prisoners. All I asked was that I be treated the same as the rest, neither better nor worse. The warden assured me that on that basis I should have no cause for complaint.

So far as I personally am concerned I have no complaint now to lodge against Warden Zerbst, his successor, J. E. Dyche, or Mr. Terrell at Moundsville, all of whom treated me fairly and humanely.

One day a prisoner found pasted on the wall of his cell a quatrain, anonymously written, which he copied and gave to me. I put it in here not only as indicating the poetry that is often discovered in the hearts of some prisoners, but as a passionate appeal which all of them make for

those opportunities in society which are so often
ruthlessly denied them:

> "Oh, oft the sky's most glorious blue
>   Smiles through the captive's cell,
> For he alone of heaven can think
>   Who dreams through nights of hell."

CHAPTER IV.

Sharing the Lot of "Les Miserables".

In the preceding chapter reference was made to my cell and cell mates. To be more specific, I was lodged in Cell No. 4, Range No. 7, Cellhouse B. In this limited space I soon began to feel that we had to set up a little world of our own.

Cut off almost completely from the outside world and from all former activities, the problem of what it was possible to do that would be helpful or of some service to my fellow prisoners as well as myself arose, and I found myself occupied in making a daily program and endeavoring to carry it out. I missed greatly the papers, magazines and other literature I had been receiving and reading. All this was completely excluded by order, I was told, of the Department of Justice. This order was not revoked until a few days before I left the prison. The issue was raised at that time with the department at Washington by some of the more influential publications which had been excluded, and whose publishers demanded to know upon what authority papers that were received and transmitted through the mails were intercepted and prevented from reaching their destination.

Not a socialist or radical paper, or magazine,

or book addressed to me was allowed to reach me until the revocation of the order that came near the expiration of my term. These papers, when they arrived at the prison, were torn up and thrown into the wastebasket. Parts of them were sometimes picked out and pieced together by some prisoner employed in the office when they contained something that he thought might especially interest me, and he would hand these scraps to me in the stockade.

For reasons not necessary to explain the prison authorities took every precaution to have socialist and radical literature excluded from the prison, and in this they were no more successful than in keeping out "dope" and other contraband articles.

As my cell became my world, and I understood its limitations, it began to expand and I so adapted myself to my prison situation that the steel bars and gray walls melted away. I set myself at liberty in a way to demonstrate, to myself at least, the triumph of the spirit over the material environment under any possible circumstances. During the day I was at my work in the clothing room where I came into intimate contact with a number of young prisoners, some of whom were having their first taste of prison life, and with whose co-operation the simple duties exacted from me were performed in a spirit of mutual sympathy which afforded me, as I believe it did them, great satisfaction.

Just after being assigned to the clothing room I had my first brush with prison guards. Here let it be said that some of the guards are decent and humane fellows who treat the prisoners with all the consideration the rules will allow, but there are others who are scarcely a degree above the brute and wholly unfit to have authority over helpless prisoners.

There was one in particular whose duty it was to escort the prisoners to the stockade. He was ashamed of his club and refused to carry it. I never once saw him with a club in his hands. The hundreds of men he had in charge held him in high esteem and they were the most perfectly behaved body of men in the prison.

The incident which I am about to relate occurred in front of the building in which I was employed. The isolation building to which prisoners under punishment are committed was near by. The rules forbade any communication with them by sign or otherwise. All of the prisoners in isolation were interested in me and would watch for me to pass their grated windows. One day one of them called me by name and waved his hand in friendly recognition. I waved my hand in return.

There and then I had committed a grave offence against the prison code and was myself due for a course of bread and water diet in isolation. A guard rushed at me like an infuriated bull, upbraiding me and taking my number. I calmly told him to report me as he had threatened to do, saying that if I had violated a rule I was prepared to take the consequences the same as any other prisoner. The report of the incident rapidly spread among the other prisoners and great excitement prevailed for a time.

Would they put me in the "hole"? That question was repeated on every tongue. I neither knew, nor did I care. I wanted what came to all the rest of the prisoners under the same circumstances, whatever that might be. The guard reported me to the deputy warden, and the latter to the warden, as I was told, but nothing came of it. It was my first reported infraction, and the reader may judge as to the gravity of the offence.

Mealtime always presented a lively scene in the general mess. Twenty minutes were allowed at table and conversation was permitted during the period. Breakfast, dinner and supper were served at about 7, 12 and 5 o'clock respectively. After supper we marched to our cells and there we remained until the breakfast hour the following morning. Fourteen consecutive hours every day in the week to be locked in a cage with five other men is a long and monotonous siege, as any prisoner will testify.

At Moundsville the prisoners were given an hour of recreation in the yard after their supper before being committed to their cells.

On one of his regular trips of inspection of Atlanta Penitentiary Denver S. Dickerson, former superintendent of federal prisons, came to see me after he had concluded his business with the prison, and in our interview I asked him why the same arrangement could not be made there that they had at Moundsville. I pointed out what a benefit it would be to the prisoners and what a good moral effect it would have upon them, especially during the sweltering days of the long southern summer.

He agreed to see what could be done about it when he returned to Washington. To my great satisfaction the order was issued and became effective with the beginning of summer and remained so during the entire season. Each evening all save those in solitary confinement were given the freedom of the ball grounds where prisoners may spend Saturday and Sunday afternoons, and holidays. For some reason the concession was allowed only that one season. I was told it was not renewed because of the inconvenience occasioned to the guards by having to do extra duty during that interval.

The evening hours spent in the cell were devoted mainly to reading and conversation. Every conceivable subject was brought under discussion, and I was benefited as well as surprised by the wide range of worldly knowledge possessed by my fellow prisoners. One of them had travelled extensively in Europe, as well as in this country, and had an unending fund of information and experience to relate. Each of the others had his own stories to tell, and here it may be said that every man in prison embraces in his person a volume of biography in which the tragedy of life is written in agony and tears. In the humblest among them there is in his life's story and his failure to overcome the odds against him a dramatic element that makes him a study well worth while to any one who loves his fellow man and wonders why he happened to be marked by the fates to have his life—the most precious thing of all he possesses—wasted in a prison den.

The cell in which I had settled assumed the institutional form of a perfect little democracy. We had all things in common—or would have had if we had had the things. This reminds me of a little anecdote related by one of the convicts.

Two tramps who had spent the night together in a box-car were wondering how and where they were to get their breakfast.

"What will we have to eat this morning"? asked the first one, whose sense of humor had not deserted him.

"Well", replied the second one, "if we had ham we would have ham and eggs, if we had the eggs."

But speaking seriously, I was never more free in my life, so far as my spirit was concerned, than I was in that prison cell. There was never a harsh or an unkind word spoken in that little community. When the lights were switched off at ten o'clock, and we had to retire whether we felt like sleeping or not, we bade each other good night just as though we had been intimates all of our lives.

The incentive to greed which dominates in the other world was lacking there, and human nature, unalloyed, had a chance to express itself, and it did so in a spirit of mutual kindness and understanding which greatly impressed me and which I shall never forget.

These men were convicted felons, outcasts from society, pariahs, and yet in their ministrations to me and to each other in their unselfish desire to give rather than receive, and in their eagerness to serve rather than be served, they set an example that might well be followed by some people who never saw the inside of prison walls.

In our cell in the great Federal Penitentiary from which the world was shut out we were alike branded as criminal convicts, but in the little community that we had set up in that cell there was not the slightest trace of a criminal, and the brotherly relation to each other, and the condition from which it sprang precluded the possibility of crime or criminal intent from entering that voluntary prison brotherhood.

The prison food was the one great unending source of complaint. The same is true to a greater or lesser extent of every jail and prison in the land. There was no lack of food at Atlanta so far as quantity was concerned. The bread was the one item about which no reasonable complaint could be made; as for the rest, it was the cheapest and stalest conglomeration of stuff that the market afforded. Coupled with this was the fact that the food was never properly cooked, but steamed and stewed. Even had it been of better quality when it left the market-place, it would have been rendered unedible by the steaming process. This ill-cooked stuff was served in a manner to cause revulsion to all alike, and that item in the prison life aroused more ill-feeling and resentment than all other causes combined.

No satisfactory system of feeding prisoners, free from graft, peculation and other corrupt practices known to prison institutions has ever yet been devised so far as I know. The usually accepted theory is that anything is good enough for jailbirds and convicts. That inhuman attitude which is part and parcel of the prison discipline is shared by society, any of whose members may at any time become convicts either for breaking the law or for upholding the law in time of public excitement as well as in popular tranquility. Whatever modification there may have been in the barbarous punitive theory in relation to offenders against society that system is still stoutly upheld and vindicated in the wretched menu and table service of every prison in the land.

It is extremely difficult to say whether men who go to prison are ruined more quickly physically by the rotten food served to them, or morally and spiritually by the harsh and bitter treatment they receive. Whichever method of degradation comes first in the inevitable prison process of human deterioration, it can be said without fear of contradiction that they are twin evils in reducing men to caricatures.

To feed prisoners decently and wholesomely, not extravagantly, but in a clean, plain and substantial manner to conserve their health instead of undermining and destroying it, would do more to humanize the prison and to make it reformatory, rather than a deformatory, than any other one thing that could be suggested in the prevailing social system. But as to the necessity of the prison at all I shall have something to say in a later chapter.

Such a system, however, will never be established until direct and effective measures have been taken to eliminate the graft of one kind and another in the contracts under which the food is furnished, and in the handling of the food inside the walls from the time it is delivered until it is served to the convicts.

As a single typical instance I may relate the following incident:

It was commonly understood that there was a regularly organized traffic carried on in the prison kitchen at Atlanta in which the choicest foods were privately sold and disposed of under the government's roof. Two of my cell-mates had told me that they knew of two employes in the kitchen who had bought their jobs at a hundred dollars each. In their positions they were able to realize handsomely from the foodstuffs that passed through their hands by selling it to favored prisoners in exchange for tobacco, which, in prison, is equivalent to legal tender in the outer world, and for cash when they could strike a bargain either inside or outside, which was frequently the case.

Realizing that the general run of the prisoners were the victims of this arrangement, and that they were not getting the food the government was paying for, I reported the matter to Superintendent Dickerson on his next visit and had him confronted with the men who made the charge; those men came before Mr. Dickerson and named the purchasers and the sums they had paid for their kitchen jobs.

Mr. Dickerson made notes of the evidence and said the matter would be investigated. On his leaving the city the two men who gave the testimony and exposed the corrupt practice were reduced to menial positions, and thus were made to pay the penalty for exposing one of the vicious abuses that obtain within prison walls.

The stockade at the Atlanta prison in which prisoners enjoyed their brief season of comparative freedom afforded excellent opportunity for the study of human nature as it is influenced by prison life. Each day, when the weather permits, the prisoners, save those in isolation, are permitted an hour in the stockade to which they are escorted in relays by their respective guards.

On Saturday and Sunday afternoons when the entire body of prisoners were allowed the freedom of the ball park, the social life of the prison found its most interesting expression. All sorts and conditions of men mingled freely there—men charged with every conceivable crime, and generally regarded as dangerous criminals. Yet, I never saw a more orderly and well-behaved crowd of people in the outside world.

When I appeared among them it was a continuous reception until the bugle called us back to our cells. Scores of these prisoners had been waiting during the week for the opportunity to tell me their stories, to examine the papers in their cases, to read their letters, and to give them counsel. My time among them was wholly taken up in this way and often I was unable to give attention to all who wished to see me.

It was in this way that I came to know intimately the men in prison, the kind of men they were, how they came to be there, and their reaction to prison life. It was to me a sympathetic study of such intense human interest that I say deliberately that I would not exchange the years spent in prison for any similar period in my life.

It has been my conviction since having had the actual experience that only the inmate, the imprisoned convict, actually knows the prison and what it means to him and his kind. Even the officials in charge and on the grounds, and in close personal contact with the inmates, do not know the prison. Indeed, they cannot know it, for they have never felt its blighting influence, nor been oppressed by its rigorous discipline; nor have they suffered the mental and physical hunger, the isolation, the deprivation and the cruel and relentless punishment it imposes.

If one could read what the iron fist of the prison traces in the heart of its inmate, what is registered there in bitterness and resentment, he would know more about the prison than he could ever learn in a life time as a mere observer or even as an officer in charge.

Many persons visit prisons and imagine after being conducted through its corridors and over its grounds that they have learned something about that mysterious institution; not a few of them are impressed with the plaza at the front of the reservation and with other external features intended to relieve the grimness of the gray walls and steel bars. They conclude that the state has provided a comfortable resort and has done handsomely by the criminals who are confined there.

As a matter of fact, they have been permitted to make but a very superficial examination and have been shown only such parts of the institution as were most likely to impress them favorably, and to send them forth commenting upon the humaneness with which the state treats its prisoners.

Had these visitors and others, who complacent-
ly accept the present prison as the final solution
of the crime problem, been obliged to spend a
month within the walls, submit to the iron discipline enforced there, eat the nauseating food,
and feel themselves isolated, cramped, watched
day and night, counted at regular intervals, and
dwarfed and dulled by the daily deadly routine,
they would undergo a radical change of opinion
in regard to the lot of men and women who are
caged like animals by human society.

CHAPTER V.

After spending two months in a cell during the blazing hot summer of 1919, and starved rather than nourished by the food, I was reduced to almost a skeleton. My normal weight is 185 pounds, but at the time of my transfer to the hospital I weighed less than 160. Reports as to my being in a critical condition reached the outside world, and the warden received frequent inquiries both from the press and my friends concerning my health.

It was at this time that the press in Atlanta received advices from New York that I had been reported dead. The warden was besieged with inquiries by telephone and otherwise. Not contented with his assurance that I was alive, the press representatives came to the prison and would not be satisfied until the warden sent for me to appear before them and contradict the report of my demise. But it must be confessed in all candor, that in all but the spirit there was scarcely enough left of me to make a successful denial.

Having heard these alarming reports, my comrades in Ohio, from whence I had been sent to prison, asked Mrs. Marguerite Prevey, who had been one of the signers of my bond in the federal court at Cleveland, to come to Atlanta to make a personal observation of me. Mrs. Prevey appeared to be greatly shocked when she saw me and noted the change that my physical condition had undergone in prison. After my interview with her, unbeknown to me, she saw the warden, and as the result of her talk with him I was ordered transferred to the hospital that same evening.

Upon being advised of the order I protested and endeavored to see the warden to have it revoked, but he had already left for his home. The recollection of my former reception at the hospital when I went there for examination on being admitted to the prison lingered to remind me that I was not welcome there.

That evening in the hospital I had a brusque interchange with Mr. John C. Weaver, the prison physician, who, I felt had not a sympathetic feeling for me. But subsequently we came to a mutual understanding and were on most agreeable terms all the time I was there. The following morning Dr. Weaver explained in a friendly way that I had been ordered to the hospital where I might have the care and attention that he said my condition required, and that I would soon realize the change was to my advantage. Dr. Edgar S. Bullis, who at that time was the assistant physician, had said, in answer to an inquiry, "Debs may die any minute". This report reached the Department of Justice at Washington and a telegraphic order was issued by Attorney General Palmer for a special examination and for an immediate report of my condition.

My heart action was weak on account of the low state of my vitality, and this was the exciting cause of the alarming statements that eminated from the prison. Just what kind of an official report was issued in my case the rules did not permit me to know, but I could not help wondering why on two separate occasions special information as to the state of my health was ordered from Washington, knowing that, save in a single instance which is too well known to merit mention here, no prisoner had ever been released from Atlanta on account of his physical condition, or because of the probability of his dying there. Many inmates died in the prison hospital while I was there. Some of the cases were too pathetic for words. Mothers, fathers, wives and children often entreated in tears that their beloved might be returned to them and allowed to die at home rather than in prison with its attendant disgrace to the bereaved ones. But all in vain!

I recall a number of particularly tragic and heartbreaking instances. There is space to relate but one of them.

A fellow prisoner of exceptionally fine fibre, with whom I became quite intimate, was taken seriously ill and brought to the hospital. He was

a man of refined nature who loved music, literature, children and pets. We had spent some very
agreeable hours together. This was his first
offence against the law, and he became a convict
as the result of an unfortunate business trans-
action, his lawyers having completed his ruin.
No man could possibly have been more out of
place in the role of a convict than this gentle
soul. He was eligible for parole, but it was denied him.

I should like to observe here that in the matter of parole the granting of some seems as
strange as the refusal of others to those who do
not know the hidden hands that pull the wires
behind the scenes. Money and political influence are frequently determining factors in
such issues.

This afflicted prisoner made a special appeal
to the superintendent of prisons that the parole,
to which he was eligible, might be granted so
as to enable him to undergo a very necessary
operation at a hospital in New York, his home.
His request was denied.

At this time the superintendent of prisoners
was a minister of the gospel.

The wife of the prisoner went to Washington
and made a tearful plea to the Department of
Justice, but to no avail. Resigned to his fate,
the prisoner submitted to an operation in the
prison hospital in a most downcast frame of mind
and spirit.

Before going under the surgeon's knife he asked me to write a telegram to his wife, reassuring her as to the operation being successful and giving promise of speedy recovery. I wrote the telegram and it was sent in accordance with his wishes. The next morning I tip-toed into his room and found him ghastly pale, scarcely breathing, and unable to speak. In calling on him I had violated a prison rule which forbids a prisoner going into the room of another convict. My instinct of common humanity compelled me to persistenly violate this senseless rule all the time I was there. That evening my friend was dead. The report came to me as a painful shock, though it did not surprise me. It would have required a contented, peaceful state of mind for a man to have undergone such an operation successfully outside of prison. In this man's depressed condition the surgeon's knife only sealed the doom that was already upon him.

His wife and children, a beautiful family, were heart-broken. The tragic scene that was enacted behind those grim, gray walls when the wife came to claim the body of the beloved husband and father cannot be described here. It was but one of the many unspeakably moving incidents of prison barbarity.

In many cases there are no loved ones to gently bear the convict's body back to the homestead and the remains are unceremoniously carted to the weed-grown prison burial ground to vanish in that forsaken enclosure from the scenes of men and there foil ignominy and disgrace by rotting away in oblivion.

A prison hospital appeals not only to sympathetic study by its many pathetic aspects, but it excites all the emotions of the soul of a sensitive human nature. I still feel the stab of pain I experienced on bidding my last farewell to my mates, one in an adjoining room, his loyal wife sitting by his side and the eyes of both filled with tears; another close by suffering from locomotor ataxia; another with an arm gone and still another paralyzed—and so on, in all the rooms and wards surrounding me. Such suffering, misery, helplessness and despair! What pen or tongue could do it justice? The wails of agony, the groans of despair echoing through those sepulchral corridors the long, interminable nights through! I can still hear them and they awaken me from my slumber.

Not only are these suffering wretches convicts, but they are the diseased and maimed inmates of a hospital within the prison. These indescribably hapless victims are imprisoned in a double sense. I have seen men die in there under circumstances that would move a heart of stone and bring tears to the eyes of those not easily moved by another's woe.

One of the most harrowing aspects of the prison hospital is the drug addict whom I learned to know there in a way to compel the most vivid and shocking remembrance of him to the last of my days. It is incredible that a human being mentally and physically afflicted should be consigned by a so-called court of justice in a civilized and Christian nation to a penitentiary as a felon, there to expiate his weakness; and yet, hundreds of these unfortunates were sent to Atlanta prison while I was there, and ofttimes I had to bear witness to the horror of their torture when they were summarily separated from the drug they craved.

I have seen these addicts seized with the madness and convulsions peculiar to their condition, and which are terrible even in memory. As many as a score and more of these drug victims were brought to the hospital at once, and the first few days of some of them were filled with all the ghastly and gruesome writhings, shrieks and entreaties, and all the hideous torments ever conjured up in the infernal regions.

One young man, who occupied the room next to mine shortly after I entered the hospital, involuntarily compelled me to share his agony and torture. For the first week or more he could not eat a morsel of food, nor be at rest a moment. His eyes rolled in their sockets, he raved like a madman, tore his hair, swore and prayed by turns, begged to be saved one moment and pleading for death the next—all this excruciating agony for just one "shot of the dope" for which he would have bartered his soul to the devil.

This lad was under what is called the "cold turkey treatment", the drug being entirely cut off in accordance with the rules of the prison. The pity I felt for him and for others in a more or less similar condition made me ill. Night after night there was no sleep because of the suffering and outcries of these wretched creatures.

Blame them as one may, how is it possible in good conscience to punish them for their awful affliction with a prison sentence as if they were common felons. They are sick people who require special treatment, and not vicious ones to be sent to the torture chamber of a prison, and it is nothing less than a reproach to society and a disgrace to our civilization that this malady is branded as a crime instead of being ministered to as an affliction, which it most assuredly is.

It would be quite as rational and humane to send men to the penitentiary and make them slaves of the galleys because they happened to have cancer or consumption as it is to sentence and treat them as criminals for being addicted to the use of drugs.

In the light of such crude and barbarous misapprehension of the evil itself, and the utterly stupid and unscientific way of dealing with it, we may well stand appalled as we contemplate the startling and menacing increase in the number of "dope fiends" all over the United States.

Very shortly after I entered the hospital a brutal and bloody assault was made by a hospital guard on passing a prisoner who was not an inmate of the hospital. The attack was utterly without provocation. This guard, for reasons of his own, appeared to be especially kind to me, but a terror to the other prisoners. With a blow of his club he felled his victim who cried aloud that he had done nothing to warrant the assault made upon him. The blood streamed from the wound in his scalp.

The warden soon heard of the incident and hurried over to the hospital to investigate it. He came to see me at once and I told him what I knew of the outrage. I had not witnessed the attack, but I had heard the thud of the club and the prisoner shriek from pain.

Let it be said to the warden's credit that he discharged the guard instantly and the latter left town that night, it being reported that some of his previous victims were laying for him to avenge the brutalities they had suffered at his hands. He was never again heard from at the prison.

At the time this guard was removed I ventured to recommend a certain other guard to fill the vacancy. He was appointed and has been there ever since. After this incident occurred there was a most radical change in the temper and morale of the prison hospital. The terrorism which had previously prevailed ceased, and from that time forward there was an entirely different moral condition and a different relation between the guards and inmates of the hospital.

I was permitted by implied, if not by expressed sanction of the prison officials, to serve and minister to the sick and afflicted prisoners. I wrote for them the letters they either could not write, or were too ill to write; filled out their pardon, parole and commutation blanks; interceded for them whenever possible; gave them counsel and advice when they sought it, and in the intervals when we sat and smoked in the "sun parlor" we had many an hour of mutually heartening communion together.

How often they brought me their letters, either because they could not read, or because they wished me to share in the grief or gladness that might be contained in the missives from home! I have often since thought that if I but had possession of the letters received by prisoners at Atlanta which I was permitted to read, and these could be printed and bound they would present a volume of prison literature that would make the gods themselves cry out in protest against the shocking cruelties now perpetrated upon the innocent families of the convicts, to say nothing of the prisoners themselves under the present harsh, cruel and callous regime that obtains in every penal institution in the land.

CHAPTER VI.

VISITORS AND VISITING.

The circumstances under which visitors are permitted to see a prisoner are such that I did not encourage my friends to come to see me. On the contrary, I had too much respect for them to wish to have them subjected to the rules of the prison governing visits and visitors.

The visiting privilege is a very restricted one in the average prison and Atlanta is no exception to the rule. From thirty minutes to an hour is the time allotted. Persons coming to see their friend or loved one in prison are likely to be shocked by the rude manner in which they are received by the guard at the main gate of the prison.

At Atlanta a visitor must first pass two outpost guards stationed on the reservation like sentinels. These guards are armed with Winchester rifles, and as a visitor approaches the main walk the guard comes out from his solitary barrack and inquires his business. This is purely perfunctory on the part of the guard for the visitor invariably is permitted to pass on. The second sentinel is quartered directly in front of the main entrance to the prison. He also inquires as to the visitor's business, and scrutinizes him to see if he carries a camera or weapons, although no search is made of the visitor.

By this time our friend from the outside world has been impressed that he is about to enter a prison, the inner workings of which are dark and forbidding. Before the gate is opened to admit him a guard peers through the bars and asks what is wanted. If he is satisfied that the call is a legitimate one he will open the gate; if not, the visitor is sent away.

Once inside the penitentiary, the visitor is escorted to a little desk in the main corridor where he fills out a small blank, stating the name of the prisoner he wants to see, his own name and address, and the reason for his calling upon the inmate. The guard takes this slip and writes the registration number of the convict in one corner. Then a hurried inquiry is made by the guard to ascertain whether or not the particular prisoner has had his quota of visitors for that month. If he has, the new arrival is told that he cannot see the prisoner for that reason. In cases where the visitor has come from a distance, and can show that he has peculiarly personal reason for his visit an appeal may be made to the guard who, in turn, may obtain sanction from the warden, or some other higher official, to grant the interview. In cases of this kind the prisoner is always impressed with the fact that a special dispensation of justice has been made in his behalf.

A convict runner or messenger always stationed

in the corridor beyond the second gate takes the slip from the first guard and goes to call the prisoner, wherever he may be, who is merely told that his presence is wanted in the office of the captain of the guards. A prisoner so informed does not know that he has a caller awaiting him, and on the way to the office he has often conjured up in his mind some form of punishment that is about to be meted out to him for reasons that he does not know. This suspense is not long, however, for he is escorted from the captain's office to one of several reception rooms where interviews with prisoners are permitted.

The visitor waiting in the corridor is now notified that the interview is about to take place, and he follows a guard into the reception room where the prisoner is sitting on the far side of a long, plain table. The room is perfectly bare, and barred at the windows. The visitor must sit on the opposite side of the table and keep his hands in view of the guard who sits at the head of the table and overhears every word that is said, and sees that nothing passes between the prisoner and his visitor. To prevent the latter the table has underneath it a partition that extends down to the floor. No writing, not even a scrap of paper is permitted to be handed to the prisoner until it is first inspected by the guard who may or may not permit the convict to receive it.

A rather humorous incident is recalled here.

A friend came to see me and brought a letter that
he wished me to read. He attempted to pass the
letter to me, but the guard snatched it from his
hand saying, "Here, let me see that". He examined the document critically, but it was apparent that he could not read it, and he had to
pass it to my friend and have it read to him.
The exceedingly stupid expression upon the face
of the guard while the missive was being read to
him indicated the grade of intelligence that is
placed and kept in a federal prison under civil
service regulations.

There are men in prison who will not permit
their wives and daughters, or, in fact, any woman
for whom they have respect, to come to see them.
The reason for this attitude on the prisoners'
part became apparent to the writer when he perceived the low moral state of the prison in general and some of its attaches in particular. No
man who is sentitive about that sort of thing
cares to risk having his wife or daughter made
the target of lewd and lascivious comments from
the guards or inmates. So far as any wantonness
may be manifested by the prisoners, it is at least
excusable on the ground that the manner and
method of their isolation is of itself unnatural,
and therefor gives rise to thoughts that would
not be perverted were they not caged like wild
beasts and their natural instincts repressed, and
therefore unclean.

Visitors bringing fruits, candies, tobacco or

other articles to their friends behind the bars are subjected to both surprise and disappointment. The guard takes possession of the gifts with the statement that he will have to deposit them in the office before turning them over to the prisoner; the chances are that the convict has seen the last of the articles selected for him by loving and tender hands. It requires no flight of the imagination to figure out in whose hands they have fallen, and will probably remain. Articles without number brought or sent to me by friends never came into my hands. Gifts to prisoners are considered the legitimate spoils for the prison attaches who handle them.

Incidentally, if you were a prisoner, and your friend had sent a nice pipe, or a necktie, or any other article of that kind, it would not be surprising if it did not reach you at all. Very often an inferior article is substituted for the one sent. If you have a friend in prison and you send him a fine pipe it is not unlikely that it will be replaced by a cheap pipe, and the helpless prisoner is grimly amused when he receives your letter and reads your comment about the nice pipe he is now smoking in the solitude of his cell. A number of such instances were brought to my attention. A friend of mine in Florida who is a merchant, sent me a large box containing animal crackers done up in small packages. I always gave those kind of things away, passing them around among the other prisoners, and as I opened the case I was happy in the thought that these crackers would go a long way—there appeared to be so many of them. When I had taken out the top layer of packages the layers underneath collapsed; the box had been robbed before it got to me, and had been skillfully "packed" so as to present an intact appearance.

There were a great many persons who were desirous of visiting me at Atlanta, including a considerable number of residents of that city and vicinity, but for obvious reasons it was not possible for me to see them.

First of all, as I have said, I felt a reluctance, as many other prisoners do, to have those I love and esteem subjected to the humiliating conditions imposed upon visitors by the prison regime. In the next place, my attitude from the beginning had been that I would permit the prison to confer no privilege upon me, and I had no right to expect any favors on this score. It was in consequence of this that the report went out from Atlanta that I had refused to see certain visitors. As a matter of fact, such instances were due either to my already having received the full quota of visitors allowed by the rules, or else because the visitor happened to have come under the head of a certain order that was specially issued in my case by the department at Washington, and which placed me incommunicado for a time. In this position no press representative was permitted to see me, nor in fact anyone else save in the discretion of the warden. Of this order of the department, which completely suspended my writing and visiting privileges for a time, I shall have more to say in a later chapter.

An interesting visit to me was that of the delegation of socialists composing the state convention of the party in Georgia. This visit occurred during the administration of Warden Zerbst who had given the convention special permission, upon their application, to visit me in a body. There were fully a hundred or more men and women in the delegation that came to the prison, and I was permitted to meet them in the main corridor where I was tendered their congratulations in the most loyal and devoted terms, and to which I made due response. It was to me a most impressive occasion, and I doubt if a similar incident ever occurred before in an American prison.

During the informalities the guards stood by attentively, and I felt that they were as responsive to the beautiful spirit of the occasion as their prison duty would allow. Tears glistened in the eyes of most of these comrades of mine as they took me by the hand one by one and passed out through the prison doors.

It is true that I did receive many visitors in the nearly three years that I spent in Atlanta prison. As far as it was possible, I discouraged persons from coming to see me. I knew well enough that many of my fellow prisoners never received a single visitor in all the years they had spent behind those gray, grim walls. Yet, I could not share my visitors with these neglected souls, and I wanted nothing that they could not have. I anticipate the comment that this may be purely sentimental on my part, but whether it is or not, I tried to be careful lest some favor or privilege were extended to me because of the position that I had held in the outside world, that would emphasize in the mind and heart of the neglected prisoner his own loneliness and isolation.

Among other visitors there were a number of prominent persons who came to see me, and these included Clarence Darrow, attorney, of Chicago; Melville E. Stone, former general manager of the Associated Press; Norman Hapgood, former United States minister to Denmark and publicist; Samuel Gompers, president of the American Federation of Labor, and Lincoln Steffens, author and journalist. I have known Mr. Darrow for many years. He was one of my attorneys in the federal court proceedings that resulted from the great railroad strike of 1894 sponsored by the American Railway Union of which I was president. I have had several very happy personal meetings with Mr. Darrow since those distant days, and not the least of the pleasant ones occurred when he came to see me of his own volition in Atlanta prison.

Mr. Darrow had been to Washington interceding in my behalf. He was on personal terms with Newton D. Baker, then secretary of war, and A. Mitchell Palmer, former attorney general. Mr. Darrow reported to me that Mr. Palmer had expressed himself as being more than casually interested in my case, and that Mr. Baker was not unfriendly disposed toward me.

Mr. Darrow asked me if I had any objection in his seeing what he could do in my behalf looking toward a possible release from prison, and if I had any objection to others working along similar lines with a similar purpose in view. I told Mr. Darrow that I would ask for nothing for myself, nor did I wish my friends to appeal specially in my behalf for executive clemency. I told him that I could not prevent my friends doing what they could for me, but I wished them to base their appeal and petition on the broad grounds of freedom for all the political prisoners, leaving no one out who had been sent to prison because of his opinions on a public question, such as the war. When Mr. Darrow left Atlanta he went back to Washington, and had further interviews with the higher officials there.

I met Mr. Gompers when he came to the prison, at the invitation of the warden, to deliver an address to the convicts in the auditorium of the penitentiary. Mr. Gompers was courteously received by the inmates, and their response to his remarks was appreciative and generous. After his prison address we enjoyed a brief visit in the office of the warden.

Mr. Hapgood's visit was particularly pleasant to me. He was at that time writing for a newspaper syndicate in Washington, and I followed his articles in the Atlanta newspaper that published them. I understood that Mr. Hapgood had visited me so that he might write a series of articles about my case. After an hour's talk together he left, and I was much impressed by his kindly manner, his charming personality and his sincerity in the issue that had brought him to Atlanta prison. His articles appeared a few weeks later, and I am sure they had a salutary influence in directing the public's attention to the fact that may men and women had suffered imprisonment because they had stood upon their constitutional right to hold a point of view and express it.

I had not seen Melville E. Stone for twenty-five years. At that time Mr. Stone was editor of Victor Lawson's Chicago Record, and we were brought together through Eugene Field, whose close personal friendship it was my privilege to possess. At that time Mr. Stone and I understood each other perfectly. He was on one side of many public questions affecting the interests of the common people, while I was on the other. Those are matters not to be discussed here; suffice it to say that Mr. Stone and I were personally friendly, and on the occasion of his visit with me his eyes filled with tears as he took my hand and told me that his faith in me as a man had never wavered, and that notwithstanding the fact that we were on opposite sides, he had never permitted a reflection upon me as a man to remain unchallenged.

It had been my pleasure to meet Mr. Steffens many years ago. He came to see me once in Boston during the campaign of 1908 when I was a candidate for President. His visit to Atlanta occurred a few weeks before my release, and he told me much about the political and economic conditions in Russia, where he had spent considerable time investigating and observing them. Mr. Steffens was also interesting himself in the question of amnesty for political prisoners in the United States, and we talked at some length upon that subject.

The casual visitors who came to Atlanta Prison to see the institution itself almost never failed to ask the guards to permit them to see me. Many of them must have thought I was some sort of curiosity, and I was told that not infrequently guards and even trusties were offered small sums of money by these prison tourists if they would point me out to them. In almost every case they were disappointed, for my quarters were in the hospital to which visitors were not usually admitted.

One of the rules of the prison forbids a convict from addressing himself to a person from the outside unless he is specially permitted so to do. One day I was ordered to go to the warden's office, and as I passed through the main corridor an Atlanta friend saw me and got up to greet me. I extended my hand to him, when suddenly a guard screamed at the person, seized him roughly and threatened to eject him from the prison. By the same token, I had also violated a solemn rule, but no punishment was inflicted for the infraction.

CHAPTER VII.

MY 1920 CAMPAIGN FOR PRESIDENT.

It may or may not, according to the point of view, be an enviable distinction to be nominated for the high office of President of the United States while in the garb of a felon and serving a term as such in one of its penitentiaries.

I am reminded of an editorial paragraph appearing in one of the eastern dailies at the time of my imprisonment at Moundsville which read something like this: "Debs started for the White House, but he only got as far as the federal prison". I was not the least perturbed by this comment for I knew in advance that my course led, not to the presidential mansion, but through the prison gates. I had already been the candidate of the socialist party in four previous campaigns for President—1900, 1904, 1908 and 1912.

Having had almost a million votes cast for me in the latter campaign and as many more that were not counted, and feeling that I had been more than sufficiently honored, I concluded not to be a presidential candidate again, and in the national political contest of 1916 I did not permit the use of my name in the nominations. However, in the congressional convention of my district (the fifth Indiana), which followed a little later, during my absence on a speaking tour, I was unanimously chosen as the candidate for Congress and stood as the nominee in that campaign, my supporters refusing to permit me to withdraw my name from the ticket.

When the time came for making the nominations for President in 1920 I was serving my sentence in Atlanta prison, and in response to urgent solicitations from the membership at first positively declined to be considered a candidate. Later, however, when I was assured that the nomination would be made irrespective of my views in the matter, and that it would be unanimous, I yielded to the wishes of the delegates. The nomination followed and, as predicted, was made by acclamation in the convention held in New York City.

During the year previous to the convention many of the party papers carried the slogan, "From the Prison to the White House", and I was told by many of my visitors and correspondents that I would be the choice of the rank and file of the party for President. This was an honor which I had never sought; in fact, I had my own personal reasons for not wishing to be the standard bearer, reasons which dated back to the time when I was a member of the Indiana legislature. I made a resolution to myself that I would never again be a candidate for a public office, preferring to devote my energies to tasks immediately identified with the industrial side of the labor movement. The party to which I gave allegiance chose otherwise, thus setting aside my personal wishes.

Men had been nominated for President who were born in log cabins to testify to their lowly origin, but never before had such a nomination been conferred upon an imprisoned convict. It was indeed an unprecedented distinction which had been bestowed upon me, and the reader may place his own interpretation upon its significance.

Next in order was the visit to the prison of the committee on notification, the department at Washington having granted the necessary permission for such a committee to call upon me. In due time the committee arrived, consisting of both men and women, and the ceremony occurred in the warden's office, Mr. Zerbst and other officials of the institution being interested spectators.

The nomination address was in the nature of a most complimentary tribute to which I responded in an expression of my thanks and appreciation. The occasion was altogether as impressive as it was unique and created a lively interest throughout the prison.

To have a presidential candidate in their midst was a thing the nearly three thousand prisoners had never experienced before and they seemed to feel a thrill of pride as if they, too, shared in whatever distinction was bestowed upon me, which indeed they did, for I can say in all sincerity that there is among men in prison a fellow-feeling that in some respects is less selfish and more refined and generous than that which commonly prevails in the outer world.

The representatives of the press were in the prison at the time of the notification ceremonies and gave good accounts to their readers of the very unsual proceedings at the prison. The film photographers were also in eager evidence, as is their wont, to pictorialize the event, and a few days later the scenes were reproduced on screens in thousands of motion picture theaters throughout the country. The warden permitted me to be escorted by the committee outside the prison gates where informal conversations were held, more pictures taken, and where a group of Atlanta children presented me with a bouquet of red roses caught at the stems by a splash of scarlet ribbon. In this instance, as in a number of others, Warden Zerbst exhibited toward me personally a friendliness for which I am grateful to him.

Never in all of my experience as a presidential candidate had I been so deeply touched and so profoundly impressed by the congratulations of friends as I was by those I received that day and in the days that followed from the inmates of the Atlanta federal prison. The hands, black and white, were extended to me from the cells and from all directions, while faces beamed with a warmth and sincerity that found expression from eager lips.

The little speeches made by some of these poor broken brothers of mine to whom no nomination had ever come, save that issued by the judge who pronounced their doom, voiced genuine pride and joy in the honor which had come to me, evincing a beautiful and generous human spirit that, in spite of its hardening and degrading conditions, the prison could not extinguish.

To be perfectly candid, I felt more highly honored by these manifestations of my fellow convicts, on account of their obvious unselfishness, their spontaneous and generous enthusiasm, than any congratulatory occasion I had ever before experienced. Many were the convicts of the various hues and shades of intelligence that made up the prison population who actually believed from the enthusiasm at the moment surrounded them, augmented by the items appearing from time to time in the daily press about me, that my election was at least probable, and that with my induction into the White House a new era would dawn for them and other prisoners confined in penitentiaries and jails in the United States.

My fellow prisoners were not only much impressed by the political delegations that came to see me, but they followed closely the daily papers seeking for items that might have some reference to me. When these appeared they seemed to have the effect of an affirmation of the simple belief held by many of the prisoners that I was due to be inaugurated President in the March following the election. Not a few of the more naive convicts came to look upon their liberty as being restored to them, not when their sentences would have been completed, but when I should be placed in the executive mansion.

Among the colored prisoners it was current that they were to share equally with the white convicts in whatever beneficial change that was to take place under my administration.

One of the popular comments heard in the course of the prison campaign was that I was certain to sweep every precinct in the penitentiary, and that neither Mr. Harding nor Mr. Cox, my political adversaries, would receive a single prison electoral vote.

It seems, and to my mind it certainly is, a pathetic commentary upon our social life that a faith so simple and child-like as was here manifested should have been sealed and crowned by a cruel and debasing prison sentence.

I was amused by the wit of a newspaper wag who said at the beginning of the campaign that Cox would make his speeches from the tail end of a train, Harding would appeal for votes from his front porch, while I would make my bid for the support of the electorate from a front cell. To this it was added that my political conferees would have the advantage of knowing where I stood, and that they would always find me in when they wanted to confer with me.

I was certainly saved from one embarrassment

to which other presidential candidates are uniformly subjected; I was not called upon to promise a postoffice to each of several candidates of rival factions. Neither did the matter of a presidential candidate's political expenses cause me any annoyance, for under the rules of the prison to which my campaign activities were confined, a chap, even though a nominee for the highest office, caught with so little as a dime in his pockets is ruthlessly pounced upon by a guard and the culprit haled before the prison magistrate in the person of the deputy warden and punished as if he had robbed a bank.

Not a penny is a prisoner permitted to have in his possession, and I wondered about the consternation there would be among my rival candidates for office in the outer world if they were deprived of the use of money at election time.

During the campaign the attorney general permitted me to issue a weekly statement in limited form discussing the political issues. I wrote these statements in my room in the hospital, and each week mailed them to my home in Terre Haute where they were typed and sent to the national office of the party in Chicago from whence they were distributed to the press associations and party newspapers. In this manner the convict candidate's messages were given a wide and ofttimes sympathetic reading.

Strange as it may appear, I received but two or three uncomplimentary letters during the entire campaign. The mail of nearly every candidate for an important office is burdened during his campaign with all sorts of insulting and threatening letters. One of my correspondents said that I should be shot, and the other wrote that I was at last where I belonged, and he hoped I would not leave there alive; he concluded with the hope that the warden would have my naked back lashed until it bled every day I was there. This benevolent writer also advised me in the same letter that he had written to the warden to the same effect.

Of course all these mercifully-inspired epistles were from anonymous writers who declared their implacable hatred of all things un-American, and vouchsafed their red-blooded loyalty to American ideals.

There was no attempt made at any time either by the prison officials or the department at Washington to restrict my little campaign messages. As the weeks lengthened into months I became more than ever a curiosity to casual visitors to the prison, and they employed every ruse and subterfuge with the attaches to get a glimpse of the man who had converted a federal penitentiary into his campaign headquarters.

Notwithstanding that I was clothed in the faded and frayed garb of a felon, I felt aware of a certain dignity that my peculiar position as a candidate imposed, expressive as it was of a confidence that remained unshaken in the face of all the denial it had encountered. Certainly no candidate could have been shown more respect or treated with greater courtesy than was I by the prison population and all others with whom I incidentally came into contact.

Election night is vividly recalled as a pleasant and interesting special occasion. Soon after the supper hour I was sent for and received by the deputy warden who conducted me to the warden's office to hear the returns that were being received by telephone and in the form of special messages. The warden and his wife were present as were representatives of the press. The bulletins came in rapidly and the table was soon covered with these returns.

Early in the evening I conceded the election of Warren G. Harding and my own defeat, which apparently excited no surprise among those in the office and beyond the walls; the only surprise, if not chagrin, that was felt came from the prison cells. An interesting question arose while we sat there in the warden's office as to a pardon to myself in the event of my election, and we all found some mirth in debating it. I am sure the question did not disturb my slumber in the nights preceding this particular one.

We remained in the office of the warden until the election of Harding was assured, when I once more breathed a sigh of relief as a defeated presidential candidate. I was not in the least downcast that I had not been elected President of the United States. In the next hour I was in dreamland sailing the seven seas in quest of new worlds to conquer.

The sincere regret expressed the following day by my prison mates that I had not been transferred from Atlanta to Washington by the American people would have compensated me for any disappointment I might have felt over the conduct of the campaign and its final results.

CHAPTER VIII.

A Christmas Eve Reception.

There are certain occasions in my prison experience that are vividly preserved as beautiful pictures. One of these was the celebration of Christmas Eve, 1920, in the basement of the prison hospital.

Permission had been secured by the inmates of the hospital from the officials to hold a Christmas Eve communion and spread a banquet to which the prisoners contributed the gifts that came from their families and friends. So quietly had all this been arranged, that I was in blissful ignorance of it until I was escorted to the spacious and brilliantly illuminated basement where I beheld with astonishment and delight an extended table spread with a banquet of delicious dishes that was equally tempting to the eye and palate.

Every hospital inmate who had received any gifts at all contributed them to the common lot. The holly-stamped paper in which the gifts had been wrapped was carefully preserved by the prisoners, one of whom fashioned fancy doilies out of it and spread them under each plate. The myriad colored ribbons were used as part of the festoons, and from somewhere flowers had been obtained for decorating the table. Each prisoner had brought his own little iron chair from his room or the wards, and when they were all seated they held consultation as to who should come to my room to escort me to the festive board.

Every prisoner wanted what he considered was that honor, and since the dispute could be solved in no other way they decided to hold nominations and elect an escorting committee of two. It happened that an Irishman and a Chinese were chosen. I was sitting in my own room when the two convicts came to my door and told me that I was wanted in the basement. The Irishman tried his best to appear solemn, but the face of the Mongolian beamed with anticipatory delight over the surprise that he knew would be mine in a few moments. Flanked on either side by my fellow prisoners, I walked through the silent corridors of the now deserted hospital, and down the stairs to the basement, where for the first time I realized the purpose of my being summoned. In every eye there was an expression of delight and kindness, and if I had never before understood the meaning of human happiness and the radiant heights to which it may ascend, I perceived it that night before me in the faces of my fellow prisoners who had in this loving and simple way translated the thought of "good will among men" into kindly deed.

The convict committee escorted me to the head of the table where I was informed that I was

148

their guest of honor. Sometimes there come to all of us feelings that sing in the heart and sigh for expression when only our silence really registers the depth of our emotion and our moist eyes suggest what the world could never reveal. So I cannot tell you of the deep stirrings within me as I looked down the lanes of that burdened board and beheld in the countenances of those convicts a joyous unselfishness that passes all understanding in the outer world.

I am sure my eyes never rested upon a more beautiful and inviting feast. If I had never before forgotten that I was enclosed in prison walls it certainly did not occur to me during that extraordinary evening that I was being held in custody.

In all the more than three score years of my life there had been but two Christmas eves that I spent away from home. It had been an unwritten rule in our large family to gather under the rooftree of the old home at Christmas time and spend the holidays there. It was always the occasion for a beautiful family reunion, the memory of which is treasured by me and will be "until it empties its urn into forgetfulness."

The first was in 1897 when I was filling a series of speaking engagements in Iowa, and had the detectives of the railroad companies at my heels; they followed me from point to point to assist me in my work in the way peculiar to those functionaries. This was due to my former activities among railroad men, organizing them into the American Railway Union which had sponsored the great strike of three years before, resulting, so far as I personally was concerned, in my imprisonment in McHenry County Jail, Illinois, for six months for disregarding an injunction issued by a federal court which had held me in contempt. Christmas eve, 1897, found me in Des Moines without money to pay my railroad fare and that accounts for my missing the celebration at home. The second occasion of my absence was in 1919, when I was in Atlanta federal prison.

I have mixed feelings as to the compensation that was awarded me in 1920 for my inability to be at my own fireside, but I am sure I shall never forget the manner in which my fellow prisoners exerted themselves at that prison banquet for my surprise and happiness. The scene presented aspects so unusual that I felt myself not only highly honored, but there was a silent and subtle appeal to my emotions that cannot be expressed in words.

I had never before been the recipient of such bounty, nor from such a source, nor more graciously and tenderly offered. Each had contributed his all for the enjoyment of all.

A noticeable incident that impressed me was the insistence of the prisoners to serve at the tables instead of being seated as guests. That concrete and steel-barred prison basement was a temple of spiritual fellowship in blessed re-

union that night. Seated around that hospitable
board we were brothers indeed, and I only wish
it had been possible for those who think of inmates of prison in terms of crime and degeneracy
to have looked upon that gathering of convicts
and then have been asked in what essential particular they were inferior to or different from
any similar number of human beings who were
celebrating, in stately edifices dedicated to his
name, the natal day of the Man who was born
in a stable.

It may be a fancy, but I somehow felt that
Jesus Christ was in prison that night.

Some weeks before Christmas a case containing 500 copies of a book entitled, "Debs and the
Poets", was shipped to the prison. This book
was an anthology of verse and comment collected
by Ruth LePrade and published by Upton Sinclair at Pasadena, California. It was the desire
of the author and publisher that I autograph the
books which were to be sold by them in the interest of a fund being raised to continue the agitation for general amnesty for political prisoners.
When the books arrived a copy was scrutinized
by Warden Zerbst who decided that the introduction supplied by Upton Sinclair was not particularly complimentary to the prison idea, nor
was some of the poetry. Now, although prisons
have concrete hides to cover their guilt, like all
guilty creatures they are exceedingly sensitive
as to having that guilt exposed, so a copy of the

book in question was sent to Attorney General
Palmer who ruled there was nothing objectionable in it, and that I might be permitted to autograph the copies.

At that time David Karsner was in Atlanta as
the correspondent of a New York newspaper,
and he with Samuel M. Castleton, a local attorney, who had been personally friendly to me
while I was in the prison there, asked the warden if I might be permitted to inscribe the books
Christmas Eve night. The request was granted
and the hour to begin was fixed at seven o'clock.
After the banquet in the prison hospital basement was over I went to the clerk's office where
I found Karsner and Castleton awaiting my presence. With them was David H. Clark, an Atlanta comrade, who, I learned later, had resigned his position in the post office that night
so that he might be able to join his friends in
the unusual visit with me. I recall remarking to
my friends that my batteries were all charged,
as indeed they were, for at the basement banquet
I had been called upon to deliver an address for
the occasion. I spoke over half an hour to my
fellow prisoners and I am sure I was never more
inspired to make an address than I was that
night. Several of the prisoners responded to my
remarks and I shall never forget the homely
eloquence that flowed from their honest hearts.

The books which I was to autograph were piled
on either side of me at the clerk's desk and the

work commenced. In the corridor outside a dozen or more prisoners were assembling the last of the Christmas packages for the convicts and there was an atmosphere of fellowship that pervaded the entire scene. From time to time prisoners slipped in and out of the room where I was at work to drop a kindly word, and my friends from the outside world remarked upon the amiable manner in which every convict conducted himself. Later that evening it was suggested by one of my visitors that maybe the prisoners assorting Christmas boxes would like to have a soft drink, so the matter was put up to the chief clerk who was superintending the work, and he agreed to it. Thereupon Karsner and Clark went out of the prison and down to a little store outside the gates where they purchased two dozen bottles of ginger ale.

It happened that when they asked to be readmitted to the penitentiary Deputy Warden Gregory was in the main corridor and he came to the gate to inquire what was in the box that Karsner carried.

He was told of its contents and that permit had been secured to bring it in the prison for the men who were at work over the Christmas gifts. The deputy warden felt that he should have first been consulted about the matter and he refused to allow the refreshment given to the convicts. This is but one indication of how senseless, and needlessly harsh, are prison rules. Later the deputy attempted to explain in a somewhat apologetic manner to Karsner that "who knows but that those bottles might contain 'dope' and files". This, in spite of the fact that he could have reassured himself on that score in a moment by observing that every bottle was sealed.

My visitors and I kept at the task of signing the books, every copy of which was numbered, until midnight. Then Karsner, Castleton and Clark presented me with their own inscribed copy number 65 as significant of the total of my years.

A nation-wide holiday campaign had been inaugurated for my release so that I might return home for Christmas. It has long been a custom with the pardoning power at Washington to grant a meritorious prisoner his freedom as an act of grace at the season of "peace on earth and good will among men". President Wilson granted the Christmas pardon as usual, but in this instance it was not in response to the numerously signed petitions representing every state in the union which had been presented to him, but the boon was granted to an Indian who was serving a life sentence for murder.

Attorney General Palmer had finally filed with the President his long delayed and expected report on my case. Speculation was rife as to whether the recommendation would be favorable or otherwise. The doubt was summarily dispelled when the report flashed over the wires that President Wilson had refused to grant the petition circulated and forwarded to him in my behalf, notwithstanding the Attorney General's recommendation for my release.

When Mr. Palmer's report was placed before the ailing President the latter had but one word to offer as signifying his attitude toward me. Over the face of the recommendation he scrawled, "DENIED".

I have been a trifle more than casually interested in the reason that prompted Mr. Wilson to arrive at that state of mind which is furnished by his former private secretary, Joseph P. Tumulty who, in his book, "Woodrow Wilson as I Knew Him", sets down this record of the President's comment in may case:

"One of the things to which he paid particular attention at this time, the last days of his rule, was the matter of the pardon of Eugene V. Debs. The day that the recommendation arrived at the White House he looked it over and examined it carefully and said:

" 'I will never consent to the pardon of this man. I know that in certain quarters of the country there is a popular demand for the pardon of Debs, but it shall never be accomplished with my consent. Were I to consent to it, I should never be able to look into the faces of the mothers of this country who sent their boys to the other side. While the flower of American youth was pouring out its blood to vindicate the cause of civilization, this man Debs stood behind the lines, sniping, attacking and denouncing them. Before the war he had a perfect right to exercise his freedom of speech and to express his own opinion, but after the Congress of the United States declared war silence on his part would have been the proper course to pursue.

" ' I know there will be a great deal of denunciation of me for refusing this pardon. They will say I am cold-blooded and indifferent, but it will make no impression on me. This man was a traitor to his country, and he will never be pardoned during my administration' ".

Personally I have no fault to find, nor any criticism to level at President Wilson for what he considered to be his proper course. But interest is quite naturally aroused when we come upon an expression such as the following from Mr. Wilson:

"I have no fault to find, Tumulty, with the men who disagree with me, and I ought not to penalize them when they give honest expression to what they believe are honest opinions".

I have nothing but pity and compassion for a man, even though he be President of the United States, who feels himself so unutterably lonely as to be impelled to give voice to such a sad sentiment as the following:

"It is no compliment to have it said that I am only a highly developed intellectual machine. Good God! Is there no more to me than that?

Well, I want the people to love me, but I suppose they never will.''

Immediately following the action of Mr. Wilson representatives of the press appeared at the prison for an interview, but I declined to comment on the executive's action. Some days later I was visited by two friends, one of whom was an Atlanta reporter, and during the conversation that followed I expressed my opinion of the President's action. In so doing I was entirely within my rights under the rules of the prison.

The report of my comment was published the following day and appears to have displeased the President, for immediately afterward an order was issued depriving me of all writing and visiting privileges and placing me incommunicado for an indefinite period. I was told that this measure had been taken by order of the President himself because my observations had vexed him and he wanted no more of them.

This action created a sensation in the prison and was flashed broadcast over the country. The reaction that followed was swift and emphatic. Popular resentment was far more widespread than that which attended my incarceration. Thousands of people who were not in agreement with me at all felt that my imprisonment was sufficient without depriving me of the limited rights that remained to me as a prisoner, and joined in the swelling demand that the order placing me incommunicado be revoked.

Public men of prominence and some newspapers of influence joined in the protest. So insistent became the demand for the restoration of my prison privileges that after a period of almost three weeks, during which my family and friends were permitted neither to see nor hear from me, the order was partially, and doubtless grudgingly revoked on the day before Mr. Wilson's retirement from office; but I was never again permitted to see a newspaper man or any one who was in any way connected with the press.

It was the general opinion about the prison that the revocation was deferred until the President was about to leave office and that action was taken then only because my limited privileges would almost certainly be restored by President Harding. The effect of Mr. Wilson's order of revocation increased the desire and insistence of newspaper men to see me and obtain a further expression of my views which the warden spared me under the iron-clad special rule that forbade my seeing, much less being interviewed, by reporters. The warden was kept busy enforcing the rule and a sharp lookout was kept to prevent a possible newspaper man from satisfying the public curiosity as to what I had to say about not being permitted to say anything.

CHAPTER IX.

Leaving the Prison.

The spontaneous and sensational demonstration that occurred upon my leaving the prison at Atlanta will abide with me vividly to the last hour of my life. The startling, thrilling, dramatic and deeply touching scene of that strange leave-taking is etched into my very soul. It was Christmas day. The definite order for my release had come at last after weeks and months of baseless rumors. The prison was tense with excitement. In cells and corridors, in the duck mill, in the mess room, the stockade, everywhere it was the one topic of conversation and comment. The very atmosphere seemed charged with some mysterious element, some dynamic force about to break forth to shake that formidable pile to its foundations.

The twenty-three hundred corraled convicts, so-called, of all colors, creeds and conditions, gathered there from all quarters, seemed in that pregnant, pulsing hour to typify with pathetic appeal and dramatic impressiveness, the unity of mankind, and the common brotherhood of the race.

For nearly three years I had been the daily associate and companion of these tortured souls

FEDERAL PRISON AT ATLANTA, GA., WHERE DEBS SERVED FROM JUNE 13, 1919, UNTIL DECEMBER 25, 1921, WHEN HIS SENTENCE WAS COMMUTED BY PRESIDENT HARDING.

—these imprisoned victims of a cruel and relentless fate. I had shared with them on equal terms in all things and they knew it and loved me as I loved them. They were my friends not only, but my brothers and realized and rejoiced in our mutual and intimate relations. In a thousand ways, by stealth when necessary, and by other means when possible, they made manifest their confidence and their loyalty, and coming from that pathetic source, from hearts that once beat high with hope but many of which had long been dead to the thrill of enthusiasm and the joy of life, this tender, loving tribute touched me to the heart and had for me a meaning too deep and overmastering to be expressed in words.

The hour had come when we must part. Great was its rejoicing over my release, but the parting and the uncertainty of ever meeting again struck their hearts and mine with sorrow and regret.

As the noon hour approached the Warden and Deputy Warden called to inform me that the time had come for me to take my leave. My brother had arrived to join me as I left the prison for the homeward journey. The last inmate I clasped hands with was a Negro serving a life sentence. As the poor fellow stood before me sobbing I literally saw the prison in tears.

For a moment I was rooted to the spot and shaken with emotion. I felt as if I was deserting my friends and a sense of guilt gripped my conscience.

I could see their anxious eyes peering at me from all directions, and how could I turn my back on them and leave them there! They wanted me to go, to join my family, to have my liberty, while the impulse seized me to stay with them until we could walk out of the barred cells together into the sunlight of the outer world.

It was a strange, sad, mystifying experience. As I pen these lines I live over again those solemn, heart-gripping moments. The pathetic smiles on the pallid faces that pressed so hard against the relentless bars of that living tomb will haunt me to my dying day.

What would I not have given to fling those gates of hell wide open and give to every soul therein his life and freedom!

The grim guard simply opened the steel door in front at a signal from the Warden.

The portals of the prison were soon left behind. At the edge of the reservation an automobile stood in readiness to whirl me to the depot. Flanked by the Warden and Deputy, who treated me with perfect courtesy, I was soon to greet my eager long-waiting friends and comrades.

Midway in the reservation, between the prison entrance and the street, we were halted by what seemed a rumbling of the earth as if shaken by some violent explosion. It was a roar of voices—

the hoarse voices of a caged human host that had forgotten how to cheer and gave vent to their long pent-up emotions in thunder volleys I never heard before and never shall again, for that overwhelming, bewildering scene, without a parallel in prison history, will never be re-enacted in my life.

The demonstration was spontaneous as it was startling and spectacular. No one could have planned or sponsored the sensational outburst. It all happened in a twinkling and gave the officials and guards a surprise that struck them dumb. They stood staring and speechless as they beheld the wild demonstration of the mob of convicts who but a moment before were the silent and submissive slaves of a brutal prison regime.

Feeling themselves free for the moment at least they let loose again and again in roars of farewell salutation. Prison rules, hard and forbidding, as if by magic, fled the scene, while grim guards, the pitiless terror and torment of the convicts, looked on paralyzed and speechless with amazement.

Not a word passed between the Warden, the Deputy Warden and myself as we stood rooted where we had been halted by the first outburst in the prison. We had wheeled about as one, and there we stood, mute witnesses to a scene of such tragic human appeal as would have moved a heart of stone.

My own heart almost ceased to beat. I felt

myself overwhelmed with painful and saddening emotions. The impulse again seized me to turn back. I had no right to leave. Those tearful, haunting faces, pressing against the barred prison windows—how they appealed to me—and accused me!

But I had to go. As I stepped into the waiting car and waved my last farewell another mighty shout was heard. And then another and another and still another, until far, far up the winding road and far away from the terrible prison, the last faint echo of the convict-host that wept as it cheered, died away in the distance.

CHAPTER X.

GENERAL PRISON CONDITIONS.

During the nearly three years that I was in Atlanta Federal Prison a number of convicts spoke to me from time to time of their desire and intention to escape from the prison. I invariably and emphatically advised them against it, knowing as I did, what lay in store for them as the fruit of such rashness. I also advised the men to keep within the rules and conduct themselves as decently as possible in the interest of their own protection and well-being against the cruel prison regime in general and the brutality of some of the guards in particular.

It should be conceded here that prison conditions, generally speaking, are today far better than they were at any time before in history. The truth of this is more apparent when we consider the state of the prison and its inmates in this country a century and more ago. To realize what a foul and hideous institution the prison was at that time one need only read the pages of McMasters' "History of the United States" dealing with prison life during the colonial period.

At that time men were still imprisoned for debt, and the prison sometimes consisted of an abandoned mine, a pest hole in which men and women were confined and in which they literally rotted away in filth and loathsomeness. Capital punishment would have been more merciful than the unspeakable torture visited upon the unfortunate poor who were thrown into these black holes and doomed to slow and shocking death for the crime of being poor and unable to pay some small debt.

In the progress of society, the prison has in the very nature of things undergone some improvement, but there are vast stretches yet to be covered before the prison becomes, if it ever does, an institution for the reclamation and rehabilitation of erring and unfortunate men and women.

The general public knows practically nothing about the prison and appears to be little concerned about how it is managed and how prisoners are treated. Not until the average man finds himself behind steel bars does he realize how indifferent he has been to a problem in which he should have felt himself vitally concerned.

As a rule, prisons are under the control of politicians to whom the welfare of its inmates, and the welfare of society as it is affected by them, is but a secondary consideration, if, indeed, that question really engages their attention at all. The wardenship of a federal or a state prison is, in my opinion, of more importance to society than the presidency of a college. The latter is chosen with at least some reference to his chacacter and his qualifications for the position, whereas the warden is usually awarded his office in return for his political services irrespective of his fitness to hold a position that has to do with the welfare of human beings.

The president of a college has supervision of an institution in which young and normal people are dealt with, and who readily understand and embrace the opportunity afforded them to secure educational advantages to fit them for the struggle of life. The warden of a prison, on the other hand, is in charge of and has almost absolute power over the life and destiny of thousands of human beings, some of whom are subnormal, most of whom have, for the time at least, been broken and beaten in the battle of life, and all of whom are in need of such humane and intelligent understanding and treatment as is necessary to retrieve their lost character and standing, reinvest them with self-respect and restore them to society fitted for useful service to themselves and their fellowmen.

But how many are there who take this view of the importance of the character and the fitness of prison officials, and of the function and purpose for which the prison is maintained? When it is taken into account that in the United States several hundred thousand men, women and children pass through our prisons annually and are influenced for better or for evil by their experiences in such institutions, it should appear apparent to even the most casual observer that the prison problem is one of the most vital concern to the people, and that the prison as an institution should be maintained with jealous care as to the character of the officials who are to preside over it, and as to the moral and physical treatment of its inmates.

If the people would but analyze the human equation of a prison they might better account for the crimes that are visited upon them in cities, towns and hamlets, ofttimes by men who graduated with an education and equipment for just that sort of retributive service from some penal institution.

There was a time not long ago when prison guards were armed with deadly weapons, when convicts kept the lockstep in hideous stripes, and were forbidden to speak or even look at one another. Most prisons have outgrown these abominations because it was realized that under their brutal and degrading influence men were turned into sodden beasts and subsequently settled their account with society upon the basis of the depth to which prison barbarity had sunk them.

Prison guards at Atlanta and many other penitentiaries have been divested of their deadly weapons, and are no longer permitted to bear them. They now carry clubs. In the march of prison progress we have passed from the gun to the club. I have reference here to the guards within and not those who surmount the walls, for the latter in their watchtowers are still armed with rifles and under orders to shoot to kill the inmate who may try to escape.

I must digress here a moment to say a word about the prisoner who attempts to escape. The very moment the "count", which is taken several times a day, tells of his escape, a siren, known as the "escape whistle", is blown and continues to screech at intervals for a considerable time. This is the signal for the farmers in the surrounding vicinity to rush eagerly for their shotguns and rifles and join in the mad man-hunt in which a prize is awarded to the lucky one who stalks the quarry. Fifty dollars, dead or alive, is the reward paid for the capture of the escaping convict, and I have been told that those who participate in it find it more exciting than a fox chase.

I shall not stop to comment here about my personal views as to the elevating influence of sportmanship of this nature. It is nothing less than folly, and ofttimes suicidal, for a prisoner to attempt to escape, whatever the temptation may be, for it is next to impossible for him to make his way through the lines. If he should yield to the natural impulse to break the bonds that hold him in captivity and is recaptured he must pay the severest penalty for his ill-advised attempt.

The guns on the walls that surround the prison accurately, though unwittingly, index the true character of the penitentiary in our day. It is a killing institution in a moral as well as in a physical sense. It is designed to break men and not to make them. If they are partly undone before they go to prison that institution will complete the wrecking process. The many expressions of bitterness, hatred and revenge I heard from the lips of departing prisoners who had served their sentences, left no doubt in my mind as to the effect of prison life upon its victims.

Ever since leaving the prison I have been haunted by those guns on the walls, and those clubs in the hands of guards within the walls. Neither the guns nor the clubs should be there. To the extent that they serve at all it is in a brutalizing way which tends to promote rather than restrain attempts to escape, and causes lesser infractions of the prison discipline.

The gun and the club are the signs and symbols of the prison institution and they proclaim its cruel function to the world.

In one of my last interviews with Warden Dyche before leaving Atlanta I took occasion to relate to him what I had seen of club rule in the prison and why I felt that the club should follow the gun out of prison. I told him that only men should be allowed to serve as guards who could control the prisoners in their charge through respect for their character instead of through fear for the clubs they carried. A man who can command the respect of other men only because he holds a club in his hand is totally unfit to be in any position of authority in the outside world, much less so in a prison.

After associating freely with those convicts, day in and day out, I knew beyond any question of doubt that they could be kept in far better order, that their deportment would be improved, and the morale of the prison made higher without the club to remind them that they were under its rule and were subject at any time to its use in regulating their conduct.

One day we were marching back into prison after being out in the yard. A few feet in advance of me an undersized and emaciated convict was shuffling along in the line. It was rather warm and his jumper was open at his neck. This was contrary to the rule, and a guard standing by gave him a vigorous punch with his club that doubled up the prisoner in pain, the guard yelling above the shriek of his victim, "Button up there!" It was with difficulty that I restrained my own feelings. I did not report the guard for the reason that I had made up my mind from the beginning of my sentence to make no individual complaints while I was within the walls, having concluded it would be better policy to accept the situation as it was, and bide my time until I should be free to register my opposition to the whole prison system.

Another personal experience with a brutal

prison guard is recalled. It was on a Sunday morning in the prison chapel where I had gone to join the other inmates in attending devotional exercises. At an appointed hour the prisoners march into the chapel which is on an upper floor of one of the main buildings. The inner blinds were partly closed and the room was rather dark. As we filed in, I stood for a moment at the end of a row, not knowing until the men in advance of me were seated if I was to occupy that row or the one behind it. In that moment of innocent pause I excited the wrath of a guard who was standing by swinging his club. I do not know if he knew me, nor does it matter. I only know that he howled loud enough to be heard a block away, "Sit down there!"

I felt that it was the club rather than the brute in the man that had proclaimed its authority. I did not resent the outrage, for I never permitted acts of that kind to insult me, or to disturb my equanimity, which I managed to maintain throughout my nearly three years in Atlanta prison, as a convict of the United States Government because I delivered a speech during the war expounding the cause of universal peace on earth and good will among men.

Hundreds of stories of the experiences of others along similar lines reached me whenever the inmates had a chance to tell me of their troubles, and what they thought of the guards, the clubs, the rules, and the prison in general.

The rules of the average prison are evidently framed by men who have but a superficial knowledge of the prison, and but vague and indefinite ideas of the way it should be managed for the good of its inmates and society. The one dominating purpose of these rules is repressive and the stupidity in framing them is crowned with the statement that they are expected to be "cheerfully obeyed". No prison rule was ever cheerfully obeyed, and no work done under such rules as prevail was ever cheerfully accomplished.

On the contrary, the work that a man does under the club of another is grudgingly and sullenly done. There is no joy in a prison task. Work behind prison walls is slavish in its very nature and is done only under protest. No intelligent attempt has yet been made to organize a prison on a scientific and humane basis to achieve the best possible results under the best possible conditions.

The very walls of the prison buildings betray the convict labor that reared them. The bricks in their lack of proper laying and the irregular spaces that lie between them all denote a kind of protest against the conditions under which work is done while guards with clubs in their hands stand by and watch.

Every prison is infested with that lowest of mortal creatures—the stool pigeon. In prison parlance he is known as "the rat". The stool pigeon seems to be a necessary part of a prison under club rule. Human beings ruled by brute force resent and resist and properly so, at every opportunity, and they must be spied upon and watched and betrayed by their own fellow prisoners in order to be kept in subjection.

The stool pigeon is the silent ally of the guard. He noses around to see and hear what he can that he may report what he considers to be to his advantage, and what may cause those spied upon serious trouble. The stool pigeon finds his reward in immunity from punishment and in promoting his chances for the favorable consideration of his application for pardon, or parole, or commutation. This particular subject was the source of frequent comment among the prisoners during my term.

The stool pigeon and his encouragement in the nefarious part he plays is in itself a reproach to, and an indictment of, prison management Not for one moment should such a perverted creature be permitted to function in a prison. The service he is permitted to render betrays a condition which condemns the prison by the very means it employs as a low and demoralizing institution.

Chief among the features of the prison which mark it as an inhuman institution is the maddening monotony of the daily routine. The same dull and deadening program is set for each day, and no effort is made to relieve it by a change of any kind. Almost everything is done in a haphazard way. Prisoners are placed in positions for which they are unfitted, and assigned to tasks repugnant to their natures.

It is this daily and continuous monotony that dulls the brain of the prisoner, saps his initiative, very often in his youth, undermines his health, and lays the foundation for his physical and mental deterioration and final ruin.

CHAPTER XI.

Poverty Populates the Prison.

When we come to make an intelligent study of
the prison at first hand, which can only be made
by one who has had actual contact with convicts
and who himself has suffered under the brutal
regime that holds sway in every penal institution,
and arrive at a final analysis of our study, we
are bound to conclude that after all it is not so
much crime in its general sense that is penalized,
but that it is poverty which is punished, and
which lies at the bottom of most crime perpetrated in the present day.

In a word, poverty is the crime, penalized by
society which is responsible for the crime it
penalizes. Take a census of the average prison
and you will find that a large majority of people
are there not so much because of the particular
crime they are alleged to have committed, but
for the reason that they are poor and either
lacked the money to engage the services of first
class and influential lawyers, or because they
lacked the means through which they might have
been able to put off the day of final conviction and
sentence by postponements, continuances and
other delays, artifices and subterfuges, in the
handling of which high grade lawyers are skilled

adepts. A poor man cannot afford to pay fees to attorneys who often use their offices to dispose of witnesses whose testimony might be damaging to the cases of their clients. The poor man caught in the meshes of the law must run his chances, whatever they are, and take the consequences, whatever they may be.

It is too obvious to require special stress upon the point that there are a thousand ways in which the man with money who is charged with crime may escape at least the prison penalty from the moment that his bail money keeps him out of jail and through all the myriad technicalities his purse will permit him to take advantage of; some of these technicalities not infrequently have reference to the personnel of the jury that will try his case, and other phases of the trial which can, by the use and influence of money, be made to serve to the advantage of the man who has it.

Instances without number might be cited in support of this flagrant fact, but one will suffice for the present purpose.

Charles W. Morse, a multi-millionaire, was sentenced to serve fourteen years in Atlanta Federal Penitentiary for illegal financial manipulations involving millions of dollars. It was a rare instance, indeed, that a man of millions should be sent to prison, and it was only possible through his having come into collision with still more powerful financial interests. Now, prisons are not made to hold multi-millionaires, but only the improverished victims of their manifold manipulations.

These favored few who may appropriate to themselves untold wealth usually operate prudently within the law under expert legal advice and guardianship of the highest priced lawyers in the land. The imprisonment of one of them is an anomaly for which there must be special and extraordinary reason.

Of course Mr. Morse was not permitted to serve his sentence. From the moment the prison doors closed upon him there ensued the most unusual solicitude on the part of the government for his well being.

Very shortly after Mr. Morse entered Atlanta prison the assistant surgeon general and next the surgeon general of the United States paid him a personal visit in their official capacities. As a result of their visits, either directly or indirectly, Mr. Morse was transferred to Fort McPherson and placed in charge of two special nurses. The examining physicians then reported to the department at Washington that in prison the patient would die within three months, and that his release would prolong his life to not exceeding half a year.

Some interesting details which I possess could be added here, but a few incidents will serve the present purpose. According to common report at the prison and elsewhere, including an admission by Mr. Morse himself, fabulous fees figured in the affair. A certain lawyer who formerly resided in Atlanta is understood to have received a sum in six figures for his part in Mr. Morse's release, and he is now practicing law in New York.

Harry M. Daugherty, one of the acting attorneys for Mr. Morse at that time (1908) who was later Attorney General, also received a fee which no poor man could ever have paid for a service of which no poor man ever would have been the beneficiary. The man in the White House who issued the order that cancelled the sentence of the multi-millionaire and set him free is now Chief Justice of the Supreme Court of the United States.

It remains but to add that Mr. Morse, who was to have died ten years ago, in the professional opinion of the physicians who examined him, is still alive, and has once more come into collision with the Department of Justice at Washington in matters that are said to involve more millions.

One more similar case is here cited.

Frank Noble, a wealthy tile manufacturer, was sentenced to serve four months in jail in New Jersey in November, 1922. Mr. Nobbe, with twenty-nine other persons and nineteen corporations, was convicted on evidence obtained by the Lockwood Committee in New York City of having violated the Sherman anti-trust law. Five physicians examined the wealthy prisoner, and as a result of their report President Warren G.

Harding ordered him released from jail on January 8.

Let it not be understood that any satisfaction would come to me from seeing a rich man kept in prison. I do not believe that a prison is a fit place for any human being, rich or poor, and I would not confine my worst enemy in its cruel cages.

My feeling toward the prison from the hour I entered it was such that I rejoiced in the departure of each of those whose terms had expired, and I was saddened by the entrance of every man whose shadow was cast upon its grim portals.

If poverty, of which so many are now the helpless victims, could by some magic of power be abolished the prison would cease to exist, for the prison as an institution is cornerstoned in the misery, despair and desperation that poverty entails.

The reason I believe that the time will come when the shadow of the prison will no longer fall upon the land is predicated upon my conviction that the day will dawn when the scourge of poverty—the foster parent of ignorance, immorality, vice and other ills that afflict the children of men—will be Banished from the earth.

During my prison days I made it a special point in my contact with the convicts to ascertain to what extent their poverty, their lack of pecuniary means, was responsible for their imprisonment. The conclusion was forced upon me that an overwhelming majority were sent to prison only because they did not have money to take full advantage of the means afforded to those who possess it of escaping the penalties of the law in the prevailing system of its administration.

When I stand before the turrets and battlements of a prison I have a sickening sense that the institution is the negation of hope, the breaker of bodies, the blighter of spirits,—a scowling reproach to society and a towering menace to civilization. If any good issues from it under its present regime it is in spite of its cruel and repressive purposes and methods, not because of them.

I am wondering in this connection what I would think of myself if I inflicted poverty upon my fellow-man and then damned him for being poor by thrusting him into a steel dungeon to expiate his "crime".

When human society has become intelligent enough to realize the responsibility for poverty it will also be humane enough to refrain from punishing its victims by consigning them to felons' cells.

It is unfortunate that hitherto no scientific and comprehensive method has been devised of ascertaining and setting forth clearly to just what extent poverty is directly and indirectly responsible for crime. It may be pertinent to observe here that it is certainly not a flattering commentary upon society that so many find it easier to steal than to earn an honest living.

We know beyond all question of doubt, after the most searching investigations, that among women poverty is responsible in an overwhelming number of cases for what is known as prostitution. Is it not shocking to think, for instance, that a woman can command more money for traffic in her sex in an hour than it would be possible for her to earn in a week of legitimate labor?

The law's delay is the prolific source of not only gross miscarriages of justice, but of the most cruel discriminations against those least able to bear it. Chief Justice Taft is on record as saying that such delay is a burning disgrace to the American system of jurisprudence. Here let it be stated that the law's delay almost invariably serves the interest of the man who has money and to the disadvantage of the man who has none.

The man of financial resources has no trouble to find the legal technicalities through which almost indefinite delay finally results in his acquittal of the charges against him, or in the case being forgotten altogether. On the other hand, the man who has little money, or none at all, is juggled by cheap lawyers through the courts until his means are exhausted, and he is then kept in jail for weeks, sometimes months, all the while his presence there swelling the revenue of grafting officials.

It is in the jails where many young men are initiated into the ways of crime and are subsequently launched on criminal careers. When these men leave the filthy pest houses and come to realize the injustice they have suffered on account of their poverty, and how indifferent society is to it all, they are apt to conclude that they must find ways and means to shift for themselves, especially as they now bear the brand of Cain for life,—for having a jail record is quite as irrevocable as any other feature of their personalities.

A few days ago a young man called upon me to relate his sad story. He was a prisoner at Atlanta while I was there. He was quite young, and on his release he appeared to be deeply penitent, resolving to "go straight" for the remainder of his life. He soon obtained a satisfactory position, but after being installed in it he felt that he should be frank with his employer, whom he now came to look upon as his benefactor, and concluded that he must tell him of his prison record.

The employer was rather profuse in his expressions of sorrow for the former plight of his new employee, but told him that he could not afford to have in his employ a man who had been a convict. Some persons might think the young man was foolish in disclosing his prison record, but the chances are the employer would have heard of it anyway, and summarily dismissed him.

183

Now, what is a man to do who is not allowed to make an honest living because he has been in prison? The question answers itself. Is he not almost inevitably driven into crime and sooner or later forced back into prison by a society that forbade him from earning an honest livelihood?

Many a man has revenged himself upon society in the most gruesome and terrible manner for having been denied the opportunity to live down an error in his past life. I maintain that the state, as a mere matter of self-protection, to say nothing of its moral obligation, should concern itself directly with men and women released from prisons and see that they are provided with a fair opportunity to maintain themselves and their families in decency and comfort, and that all possible encouragement is given them to lead clean and useful lives. If this simple device were at once made effective it would, without a doubt, result in a material dimunition of crime.

But almost the opposite manner now has public sanction in dealing with ex-prisoners and convicts. It is taken for granted that they are all vicious and incorrigible. Their very sentence is prima facie evidence of their innate depravity, and they are not only marked for perpetual ostracism, but are to be pursued and hunted and hounded back into prison again as if their crime consisted in being turned back into society.

I have already referred to how the offender is pilloried in the courtroom and how he is punished there by exposure and humiliation even though he may not be guilty of the charge lodged against him. Much more could be said, also, about the foulness of county jails and the contamination of youthful first offenders who are consigned to them, and of the process whereby criminals are made and crime is spawned and fostered.

I shall conclude this chapter with a brief statement of the foulest and most abhorrent and destructive evil of which the prison is the pestilential breeding place. I shrink from the loathesome and repellant task of bringing this hidden horror to light. It is a subject so incredibly shocking to me that, but for the charge of recreance that might be brought against me were I to omit it, I would prefer to make no reference to it at all.

Every prison of which I have any knowledge, either of my own or through my observation and study, reeks with sodomy. It is the vice of vices consequent upon the suppression of the sex instinct in prison life. I am unable to state here the many hideous and unbelievable forms in which this fearful and debauching vice is developed and practiced.

I saw the body and soul-destroying effects in many of its victims and I heard tales of actual occurrence that sickened and almost prostrated me. It is this abominable vice to which many young men fall victims soon after they enter the prison—a vice which often blasts their hopes, ruins their lives and leaves them sodden wrecks.

It may be imagined that the perverted practicers and purveyors of sodomy are its only victims, but this is an awful mistake when we come to realize that the depravity visited upon these unfortunate by the prison system goes back into society to contaminate and corrupt to the extent of their own pollution.

The stream of foul language that flows from the lips of the sodomite registers unerringly the degree of the depravity to which he has sunk as an imprisoned human pervert.

Not as long as the prison is a punitive institution, and has the punitive spirit, and is under punitive regulation can this shocking and devastating evil ever be successfully coped with, or its frightful consequences to its immediate victims and their ultimate ones be materially mitigated.

CHAPTER XII.

The most vitally important phase of the entire criminal question is the creation of the criminal and launching him upon his criminal career. If the criminal were not created the prison would be unknown. If, as seems to me self-evident, the so-called criminal is a social product, it is of supreme importance that society should realize not only its own responsibility, but the necessity of making the most searching investigation of the process whereby crime is produced, and devising means to suppress or at least to mitigate the evil.

There is much said and written these days, especially by lawyers in trial courts, about criminal psychology. The subject has, in my opinion, been considerably overdone. If the criminal instinct actually exisits in the human being as a positive factor in his mental and physical organism it is so rare and exceptional as to make it a subject for pathological treatment, and only by extravagant exaggeration can it be regarded as a prevalent psychology. Most men and women who, by the lofty professional criminologists, would be charged with having a criminal psychology are simply the victims of social in-

187

justice in some form, and when the cause of this is ascertained and removed and the victims are accorded human treatment in terms of love and service their "criminal psychology" at once vanishes.

I should rejoice in the opportunity to take a dozen of the most pronounced cases wherein criminal psychology has been established by the professors who delve into the mysteries of the underworld, place them in their proper environment, surround them with wholesome influence, and give them such incentives to right living as every human being should enjoy, and then see what becomes of the "criminal psychology" with which these dozen human specimens are supposed to be afflicted. It has been a matter of such common observation with me that poverty, generally speaking, is the basis of crime that in discussing this phase of the question I am under the necessity of repeating and emphasizing such references to poverty in relation to crime as were made in preceding chapters.

I have seen boys in jail not because they had committed crime, but because they could not furnish bail for their release until the charge of crime lodged against them was proven at their trial. They were not guilty, but were presumed to be innocent, for they had not been tried. Yet, they were in jail and their poverty was therefore their crime. Many a hardened criminal of today was started on his career in some such way, as

I learned from the heart to heart stories I heard from their lips as we sat together in the shadows of the prison walls.

At this point there occurs to me a most poignant and concrete incident in relation to the point I have just made, with the exception that the case concerns a girl instead of a boy. Between the period of my sentence in Cleveland in September, 1918, and my going to Moundsville Prison to serve it in April, 1919, I made an almost daily speaking tour of the territory embraced by the federal judicial district of northern Ohio, being permitted so to do by the court that had pronounced my sentence. An appeal in my case was at that time pending before the Supreme Court of the United States.

I had filled a speaking engagement near Cleveland, after which I visited the county jail and took to several of the inmates some cigars, tobacco and confections. As I was about to leave the grim and forbidding institution I heard the shrieks of a girl, and turning around I saw a little lass, certainly not more than 16, struggling between two policemen and pleading with them not to throw her in jail because of the disgrace that she felt would come upon her mother and knew would fall upon her. I made hurried inquiry of the officers and learned that a police matron was the direct cause of the plight of this child, who had been spied upon by the elder woman when the girl, in desperate economic necessity, had solicited a man on the street and taken him to her room. There she was pounced upon by the matron, taken to the police station and from there sent to the county jail to await trial.

I had but a few moments in which to catch a train that would take me to my next speaking engagement, but I went to the office of the sheriff and left some money which I hoped would pay the immediate costs of the girl's case, and requested that if there was any change it should be turned over to her. If there had been the least human kindness, sympathy and understanding in the police matron who made the arrest after spying upon the girl and hunting her down, she would have found a way to mainfest it by cautioning the child against continuing the sad life which she had involuntarily persuaded herself to follow. It seems to me that the innate instinct of a woman would have prevented the matron from adopting the brutal and unreasoning course which she, in her infinite ignorance, probably deemed a most worthy and virtuous action.

I am not unmindful of the fact that many people will uphold the matron and will consider that she vindicated the best interests of society by causing this child to be branded not only as a common prostitute, which she was not, but stigmatizing her for the rest of her life as a woman with a police record. Between those who adhere to this point of view and me there yawns a psychological chasm as broad and as deep as that which stretches between love and hate.

No man and no women, more especially no boy and no girl should ever be put in jail for being unable to furnish bail. We declare that under our benign code a man is innocent until he is proven guilty and the next moment we lock him in jail before he is tried. If the honor of men were appealed to, and they were trusted to put in their appearance when they were needed, as was the common practice among Indians under their tribal code, few would betray the confidence reposed in them, and far better it would be should such rare instances as a betrayal of confidence occur, than that a single innocent boy should be lodged in jail and given a police record and started on his criminal career. In such a case a crime is indeed committed, a crime of cruel and tragic consequences, and society itself is the criminal.

The man with money is never the victim of such a crime. His money and not necessarily his innocence keeps him out of jail. He can furnish bail though he may be guilty, while the poor man must go to jail though he may be innocent. Yet we proudly boast that all men stand equal before the law. If this were true one of two things would follow, either men would no longer be sentenced to prison and the prison would cease to exist, or so many would be sentenced to prison that innumerable additional bastiles would have to be built to confine them.

There is not the slightest doubt in my mind that, as a general rule, the criminal is created by the society in which he lives, and his crime as a rule is rooted in his poverty; yet little intelligent attention is given to that vital and fundamental phase of crime which has to do with the creation of the criminal. Society is greatly agitated over the epidemic of crime and cries out for protection against criminals, little realizing that it is but reaping the fearful harvest of dragon's teeth sown by itself.

And what is the usual remedy proposed for combatting crime which steadily increases in spite of the church, the school and the country club? Adopt more drastic laws! Increase the police force! Pronounce longer sentences! Inflict severer punishment on the evil doers, etc., etc.,—all of which simply indicates the puerile understanding we have of this social phenomenon known as crime. All our efforts are put forth to suppress the effect while blindly ignoring the cause, and of course our efforts are futile and barren of results.

Crime, in whatever form it may make itself manifest, is traceable in every instance to a definite cause, and until the cause is removed crime will flourish and grow apace with our vaunted civilization. We deal with effects only when we build prisons for the incarceration of criminals that we ourselves have created and for whom we are responsible.

The three boys, mere children, who were convicted at Chicago some years ago as "car barn bandits", never had a home in any decent, wholesome sense of the term. They were the inevitable products of poverty and the slums. The only interest that society had in them it imposed upon them as a penalty of its own neglect by hanging them by the neck until they were dead.

Hard economic conditions under which life in its richness and fullness and beauty is denied, and under which gaunt necessity has sway, bear a greater share of responsibility for the creation of criminals and the commission of crime than all other causes combined. The young man whose wage is insufficient to enable him to marry the girl he loves feels himself tempted to take what, in his inexperienced youth, may seem as the easier way to increase his scant revenue so that he may realize his youthful dream. The girl in the city store, or the factory, whose paltry stipend barely keeps her in the actual necessities of physical existence, and whose natural desire to indulge in some of the beauty and enjoyment of life which she beholds all about her, and which are denied by virtue of her stern economic condition, is peculiarly in a position to yield to the temptation that may lead her into the district from which there is no return.

The bitter struggle for existence is accountable, directly and indirectly, for men turning criminals and attacking by lawless means the society which would lawfully allow them but a precarious and miserable existence. The arrest of a person, however innocent, is generally regarded as prima facie evidence of his guilt. Had he been innocent he would not have been arrested, so concludes the average mind, and thus he is already convicted.

Is it not apparent at a glance that the first step has been taken in creating the criminal when he is placed under arrest, a circumstance which is often heralded to the public in sensational reports from day to day? After the arrest follows the jail if bail money is lacking, as is frequently the case, and the jail is most likely a filthy den wherein the first offender receives a rude shock not at all calculated to increase his self-respect, or enchance his confidence in law and in his own future. From the jail he is taken to court under guard perhaps handcuffed, and there he is placed in the pillory as a public exhibit. Everything is done as publicly as possible for his benefit, and all this occurs before he has been tried, and while he is presumably entirely innocent.

The public does not know the secret shame and humiliation which the untried culprit is made to suffer in this round of public exhibition in which he is the involuntary star performer. He is being punished in the most cruel and harrowing manner, and yet the unthinking crowd that ogles him in a courtroom conclude that he has entirely escaped punishment unless he is sentenced to serve a term in a penitentiary.

Here let it be observed that the agony a man not utterly devoid of self-respect suffers, the punishment he endures as the result of his first arrest, his initiation as a jailbird, his advertising in the press, his exhibition in the courtroom, guarded as if he were a convicted felon, are more poignant, more terrible, and sear and scar his spirit more deeply than any prison sentence that may subsequently be imposed.

What does the man care about a prison sentence so far as his shame and degradation are concerned after he has experienced the preliminary stages of his ruin and downfall in the public and cold-blooded manner of his arrest, incarceration, trial, conviction and sentence? When he finally reaches the prison his case as a convict is settled and his status fixed as a part of the criminal element. He may be still further hardened in his bitterness and resentment, and he may become sullen and defiant as he dons his shabby prison garb, but it is almost certain that from the time he enters prison the baser qualities of his nature will be developed and find expression.

As a matter of fact, he was already branded a felon before his trial began and, figuratively speaking, he had already served his sentence before he was actually convicted.

Oh, if we were but more human in our spirit and attitude toward the wayward boy or girl, the erring and unfortunate amongst us, what infinite pain and trouble and expense we could escape ourselves, and what tragedy and grief we would spare our victims!

How far better it were to quietly caution the young against their indiscretions than to have them spied upon by detectives and matrons, trapped and seized and exposed, their good name blasted, and their future destroyed. The reason for this is that the minions of the law, not always too scrupulous in its administration, thrive in crime, hold their official tenures, and receive their emoluments and rewards from crime.

CHAPTER XIII.

How I Would Manage the Prison.

Civil service regulations have little efficiency under a corrupt political system. The farcical nature of civil service rule as it applies to the selection of minor officials and guards in federal prisons is reflected in the low character, the ignorance, brutality and general unfitness of some of these functionaries who secure and hold their tenure through political "pull" on the outside in spite of civil service reform.

The prison warden cannot remove his guards except for specific flagrant misconduct and the immunity they thus enjoy is a virtual license to them to bully and intimidate the prisoners. The fundamental evil in the present prison regime is that the institution is under the absolute control of office holders and politicians who, even if they had the inclination, have not the time to concern themselves with prison affairs.

Attorney General Daugherty, for example, who was vested by law with almost absolute power of control over federal prisons had probably never seen one of these institutions. He had the power of life and death over every one of the thousands of inmates, and yet what does he know, what could he know of his own knowledge of the prison in which they are confined, the conditions that exist there, and the many evils and abuses of which they are the suffering victims?

He had to rely absolutely upon what was furnished him in the way of information upon his subordinates who, like himself, derive their information from still other subordinates who may perhaps be thriving in, and are possibly the direct beneficiaries of the conditions which cry for correction.

The drug traffic is one of the most pernicious and shameless evils of our prison system. It could not exist without official connivance and for this reason has never been suppressed in any federal state prison. In certain instances the most sensational disclosures have been made of the traffic in "dope", organized by prison officials and attaches, whereby the inmates by submitting to gross extortion were furnished with the drugs and appurtenances for their use by the very officials who were hired and paid to suppress such abuses.

It so happens that I had an active hand in the sensational and shocking exposure that was made some years ago of the appalling conditions in the federal prison at Leavenworth, Kansas, and which created a national scandal. An official shake-up followed, for the facts were too flagrantly in evidence to be concealed, notwithstanding the tremendous political pressure from the outside brought to bear to that end. One of the high officials of Leavenworth was accused of perverted practices with the inmates and was allowed to resign. Expensive suits of clothes were made by prison tailors for political patrons of the officials. Worst of all, however, was the organized drug traffic under the control of guards and other officials who derived enormous revenue from furnishing the inmates with the "dope" with which to debauch and destroy themselves.

I was at that time one of the editors of a Kansas paper which had a national circulation. Taking the cue from certain reports which reached us, we conducted a secret investigation of Leavenworth Prison in which we had the co-operation of certain minor officials and inmates. After ascertaining the facts, we proceeded to make the exposure in a series of decidedly sensational issues. All kinds of reprisals were threatened by prison officials and politicians.

Space will not allow a detailed review of the case here, but I must at least make mention of my having been indicted in the federal court in Kansas for my part in the exposure. The intention of those who had been exposed was to clap me in Leavenworth Prison along with the rest of their victims, but they found that I and my associates were sure of our facts and that we courted the most searching inquiry. For reasons sufficient to themselves, the prison and court officials reconsidered their course and quietly struck the indictment from the docket.

Some of the prison rules must have been inspired, if not written by such humorists as Artemus Ward and Mark Twain, or such satirists as Bernard Shaw and Henry L. Mencken. I shall allude to the rules of Atlanta Prison, but there is little difference, if any, between these and the regulations that obtain in other penitentiaries.

For instance, one rule says: "You must not try to escape". This naive injunction issued in the shadow of the cold steel which bars every door and window in every solitary building within the towering walled enclosures surmounted by sharpshooters would seem to be a trifle superfluous.

Another rule to which reference has already been made, provides that inmates are expected to "Cheerfully obey all rules". Comment is unnecessary.

Still another forbids an inmate to approach an officer in addressing him within six feet of his august presence.

"You must uncover your head in respectful manner and touch your hat or cap if out of doors in addressing or being addressed by an officer or guard"—but the official keeps his hat on his sovereign head. I am wondering what Lincoln would have thought of that rule.

The prisoner who makes the mistake of getting into the wrong cell may be punished under the provision of another rule.

Personally, I not infrequently found myself

violating the important rule that my shirt had to be buttoned at the band. Most of the time there was no button at the band. It seems strange to me that pockets were allowed in jumpers or overalls, for a specific rule forbids prisoners from putting their hands in their pockets.

Prisoners are required to rinse out their mouths and keep their lips and tongues free from tobacco stains. (This rule might be extended to the outside).

Whistling or singing is in violation of another rule,—and no wonder, for what business has a song to be heard in a dungeon?

In the prison's present raw, haphazard, utterly unscientific state of management almost everything is done in a wrong, fruitless, wasteful way. There is little method and no system.

There are, in fact, in every prison a dozen or more little prisons and the inmate is subject to the regulations of them all, and not infrequently these regulations are in conflict. On a number of occasions I found myself violating the rules of one of these prisons while endeavoring to obey the rules of another.

The various departments are under control of petty officials and each is an autocrat in his own sphere. There is often clash of authority, but in a final test they all stick together for their mutual protection. And it should be remembered that not one word in the way of a report or a complaint in regard to what goes on is permitted to be sent out by the inmate while he is behind the walls.

If the prison were scientifically organized and humanely conducted prisoners would be systematically assigned to useful tasks and paid accordingly, instead of being robbed by the state and their families allowed to suffer penury and want. What possible excuse or justification can there be for the state robbing a helpless prisoner of his labor and subjecting his family to starvation?

In a great many cases the prisoner himself was guilty of no such crime against society as that which society perpetrates upon him and his offspring.

I marvel at the incredible stupidity that blinds the men in control of prisons to the redeeming power of kindness as a substitute for the destructive power of brutality. Every instinct of our nature protests against cruelty to the helpless and defenceless, yet of all places where it is most needed mercy is least practiced in the treatment of convicts. I have seen men of mild temper and gentle disposition made sullen and vicious by harshness and I have also seen the toughest specimens of "bad men" softened and made gentle by a kind word and the touch of a friendly hand. Upon this point I can admit of no possibility of a doubt as to the saner and humaner method of dealing with the prison population.

In hedging a prisoner about with stern and repressive rules to reinforce the intimidation of the frowning ways every effort is seemingly made to exclude the human element in the fraternity of prisoners and in the autocratic relation assumed toward them by their keepers. The guard and the inmate cease to be human beings when they meet in prison. The one becomes a domineering petty official and the other a cowering convict. The rules enforce this relation and absolutely forbid any intimacy with the human touch in it between them.

The guard looks down upon the convict he now has at his mercy, who has ceased to be a man and is known only by his number, while, little as the guard may suspect it, the prisoner looks down upon him as being even lower than an inmate.

I have a thousand times had this borne in upon me touching the relation of the guard and the prisoners in his custody.

Not until the prison problem in all of its various phases is recognized as if national instead of local concern can it be dealt with in a comprehensive and effective manner.

Scientific experts would find here a field of boundless opportunity for service second to none in value and importance to humanity. Plans could be formulated upon a nation-wide scale for the development of the country's resources, for the opening of highways, the reclaiming of swamp lands and desert wastes, and the construction of

203

public works of all kinds to absorb the labor of every prison inmate in a useful and constructive way so that he could be remunerated for his services at the prevailing rate of wages without coming into demoralizing competition with his fellow worker in the outer world.

This would at once create an incentive to the prisoner to do his best, to look up and to feel he was having a fair chance to retrieve himself. His wages would meanwhile support his family and educate his children instead of allowing them, as now, in penury and under ostracism, to become a charge upon the community.

But what could be done under rational control to correct the abuses and improve the conditions of the prison as it exists today? Very much indeed could be done were it not for the organized opposition of the prison power itself to any radical departure from the present corrupt, inefficient and extravagant system. Men whose positions are at stake do not look with friendly eyes upon such a change as is contemplated in this proposal.

Thomas Mott Osborne is intensely unpopular among prison officials of high and low degree, for they see in his plan of prison management the abolition of the corrupting and grafting misrule of which many of them are the beneficiaries.

Coming directly to the question of improving the prison as it exists today, the first thing I would do would be to take it completely out of the hands of politicians and place it under the absolute control of a board or commission consisting of resident men and women of the highest character, the humanest impulses, and the most efficient qualifications for their task. The board or commission should have complete and final authority over the prison, full power of pardon, parole and commutation, and in every way charged with the responsibility to the state or the community for the management of the prison.

In the next place, I would have the prison population organized upon a basis of mutuality of interest and self-government. I would forthwith remove every gun and club from within the walls and dismiss every guard. At Atlanta Prison, for example, there are about 125 guards maintained at an enormous expense and the prison could be managed far better without them.

The most efficient guards and the only ones interested in making the prison clean and keeping out "dope" would be those chosen by the inmates from their own ranks. As previously stated, any honest warden would admit that 75 per cent of the prison population consists of decent, dependable men, and with this for a foundation I would proceed to build up the superstructure of the prison's self-determination.

Wholesome, nourishing food is the vital element in the sustenance of physical life and in prison is even more imperatively necessary than in any other place, save a hospital. The federal government makes sufficient allowance for this purpose, but there is a wide space between the treasury from which the money is drawn to the table upon which the food is served, and in the present process the food deteriorates sadly in various ways before it reaches the convicts. The matter of feeding the prisoners should have the most careful and thorough supervision of the officiating board who could, without doubt, devise a method of having the food furnished that the government pays for free from graft and peculation, and cooked and served in a clean, decent and appetizing manner.

The industrial life of the prison should be organized and systematized under the direction of the board, supplemented and in co-operation with a subordinate body chosen by the convicts of the prison. It might be necessary to employ a few experts or specialists from the outside, but nearly all the minor official positions in the offices, shops, yards, cell-houses and about the grounds and walls could and should be filled by the inmates.

I would have all the prisoners congregated to hear the announcement of the proposed changes, inviting their suggestions and appealing for their co-operation and support. This would be a direct appeal to their honor, their self-respect, as well as their intelligent self-interest, and there would be few indeed who would fail to respond with gladness of heart. An overwhelming majority would give eager acclaim to the new adventure, especially if the proposal were submitted and the appeal made in a spirit of human kindness and even-handed justice.

I would have the great body of prisoners compose a parliament established for self-rule and for the promotion of the welfare and common interest of all. A code of by-laws and regulations would have to be adopted, subject to the approval of the governing body of the institution.

An executive council consisting of inmate members should be created having power to hold daily sessions to receive suggestions, to hear and determine complaints, subject to appeal to the governing board, and to have general supervision and direction of affairs within the prison. Minor bodies for special service of whatever nature could be provided for as the situation might require.

The limited space at my command prevents further amplification of my idea of prison management, but I have a profound conviction that it is fundamentally sound and practical—so sound and practical that I challenge the powers that control our prisons to give me the opportunity to put it to the test in any prison in this country. I should guarantee to greatly improve the morale of the prison the first week, to reduce the practice of immoral, health-destroying habits, and the admission of "dope" to the minimum; increase the efficiency of the service, reduce materially the expenses of maintenance, and return the inmates to society in a different spirit and appreciably nearer rehabilitation than is now done or possible to be done under the prevailing system.

I should expect no remuneration for my service, but should regard it as a contribution to society in return for my education in and graduation from one of its chief penal institutions.

In this connection I cannot refrain from expressing to my readers the conviction that the economic and social ideals which I hold,—ideals which have sustained me inviolate in every hour of darkness and trial, would, if once realized, not only reform the prison and mitigate its evils, but would absolutely abolish that grim and menacing survival of the dark ages.

CHAPTER XIV.

Capitalism and Crime.

Crime in all of its varied forms and manifestations is of such a common nature under the capitalist system that capitalism and crime have become almost synonomous terms.

Private appropriation of the earth's surface, the natural resources, and the means of life is nothing less than a crime against humanity, but the comparative few who are the beneficiaries of this iniquitous social arrangement, far from being viewed as criminals meriting punishment, are the exalted rulers of society and the people they exploit gladly render them homage and obeisance.

The few who own and control the means of existence are literally the masters of mankind. The great mass of dispossessed people are their slaves.

The ancient master owned his slaves under the law and could dispose of them at will. He could even kill his slave the same as he could any domestic animal that belonged to him. The feudal lord of the Middle Ages did not own his serfs bodily, but he did own the land without which they could not live. The serfs were not allowed to own land and could work only by the consent of the feudal master who appropriated to himself the fruit of their labor, leaving for them but a bare subsistence.

The capitalist of our day, who is the social, economic and political successor of the feudal lord of the Middle Ages, and the patrician master of the ancient world, holds the great mass of the people in bondage, not by owning them under the law, nor by having sole proprietorship of the land, but by virtue of his ownership of industry, the tools and machinery with which work is done and wealth produced. In a word, the capitalist owns the tools and the jobs of the workers, and therefore they are his economic dependents. In that relation the capitalist has the power to appropriate to himself the products of the workers and to become rich in idleness while the workers, who produce all the wealth that he enjoys, remain in poverty.

To buttress and safeguard this exploiting system, private property of the capitalist has been made a fetish, a sacred thing, and thousands of laws have been enacted and more thousands supplemented by court decisions to punish so-called crimes against the holy institution of private property.

A vast majority of the crimes that are punished under the law and for which men are sent to prison, are committed directly or indirectly against property. Under the capitalist system there is far more concern about property and infinitely greater care in its conservation than in human life.

Multiplied thousands of men, women and children are killed and maimed in American industry by absolutely preventable accidents every year, yet no one ever dreams of indicting the capitalist masters who are guilty of the crime. The capitalist owners of fire traps and of fetid sweating dens, where the lives of the workers are ruthlessly sacrificed and their health wantonly undermined, are not indicted and sent to prison for the reason that they own and control the indicting machinery just as they own and control the industrial machinery in their system.

The economic-owning class is always the political ruling class.

Laws in the aggregate are largely to keep the people in subjection to their masters.

Under the capitalist system, based upon private property in the means of life, the exploitation that follows impoverishes the masses, and their precarious economic condition, their bitter struggle for existence, drives increasing numbers of them to despair and desperation, to crime and destruction.

The inmates of an average county jail consist mainly of such victims. They also constitute the great majority in the state prisons and federal penitentiaries. The inmates of prisons are proverbially the poorer people recruited from what we know as the "lower class". The rich are not

to be found in prison save in such rare instances
as to prove the rule that penitentiaries are built
for the poor.

Capitalism needs and must have the prison to
protect itself from the criminals it has created.
It not only impoverishes the masses when they
are at work, but it still further reduces them by
not allowing millions to work at all. The capitalist's profit has supreme consideration; the life
of the workers is of little consequence.

If a hundred men are blown up in a mine a
hundred others rush there eagerly to take the
places of the dead even before the remnants of
their bodies have been laid away. Protracted
periods of enforced idleness under capitalism
have resulted in thousands of industrious working men becoming tramps and vagabonds, and
in thousands of tramps and vagabonds becoming
outcasts and criminals.

It is in this process that crime is generated and
proceeds in its logical stages from petty larceny
to highway robbery and homicide. Getting a living under capitalism—the system in which the
few who toil not are millionaires and billionaires,
while the mass of the people who toil and sweat
and produce all the wealth are victims of poverty
and pauperism—getting a living under this in-
expressibly cruel and inhuman system is so precarious, so uncertain, fraught with such pain and
struggle that the wonder is not that so many people become vicious and criminal, but that so

many remain in docile submission to such a tyrannous and debasing condition.

It is a beautiful commentary on human nature that so little of it is defiled and that so much of it resists corruption under a social system which would seem to have for its deliberate purpose the conversion of men into derelicts and criminals, and the earth into a vast poorhouse and prison.

The prison of capitalism is a finished institution compared to the cruder bastiles of earlier periods in human history. The evolution of the prison has kept pace with the evolution of society and the exploitation upon which society is based.

Just as the exploitation of the many by the few has reached its highest cultivation and refinement under present day capitalism, and is now carried on more scientifically and successfully, and is yielding infinitely richer returns than ever before, so has the prison under this system been cultivated and refined in the infliction of its cruelty, and in its enlarged sphere and increased capacity.

Externally, at least, the prison under capitalism presents a beautiful and inviting appearance, but behind its grim and turretted walls the victims still crouch in terror under the bludgeons of their brutal keepers, and the progress of the centuries, the march of Christian civilization, mean little to them, save that the prisons of capitalism are far more numerous and capacious, and more readily accessible than ever before in history. They signalize the civilization of our age by being composed of steel and concrete and presenting a veritable triumph in architectural art.

Capitalism is proud of its prisons which fitly symbolize the character of its institutions and constitute one of the chief elements in its philanthropy.

I have seen men working for paltry wages and other men in enforced idleness without any income at all sink by degrees into vagabondage and crime, and I have not only found no fault with them, but I have sympathized with them entirely, charging the responsibility for their ruin upon capitalist system, and resolving to fight that system relentlessly with all the strength of mind and body that I possess until that system is destroyed root and branch and wiped from the earth.

During my prison years I met many men who were incarcerated as the victims of capitalism. Let me tell of one in particular. This will typify many other cases with variations, according to the circumstances.

This man has spent nearly forty-eight years in reformatories and prisons. His father died when he was a child and his mother was poor and could ill provide for her offspring. At the tender age of seven years he found himself in a so-called House of Correction. There he was starved and beaten and learned to steal.

Escaping from that institution, he was cap-turned and returned. From that time on he was marked and his life was a continuous battle. He was dogged and suspected and the little time that he was out of jail was spent in dodging the detectives who were ever on his track like keen-scented hounds in pursuit of their prey. They were determined that he should be inside of prison walls. In this cruel manner his fate was sealed as a mere child. The House of Correction for poor boys and girls comes nearer being a House of Destruction.

I spent many hours talking with this victim of the sordid social system under which we live. Despite the cruelties he had suffered at its hands, he was as gentle as a child and responded to the touch of kindness as quickly as anyone I ever knew. Society, which first denied him the opportunity to acquire a decent means of living and subsequently punished him for the crime which it had committed against him and of which he was the victim, could have won an upright and useful member in this man.

As I have already stated in a foregoing chapter, I declined to attend the prison chapel exercises. There were many other convicts who lent their presence to the mockery of religious worship over which guards presided with clubs because they were compelled so to do. The particular prisoner to whom I have referred addressed a letter to the warden protesting that he did not wish to attend devotional exercises and stated the reason for his attitude. He wrote and gave to me a copy of the letter and I introduce it here as indicating that this victim of the brutality of the capitalist system, in spite of the fact that he had spent nearly half a century behind prison bars, still possessed sufficient manhood and courage to assert himself in face of his cruel captors.

The letter follows as he wrote it:
"Sir:

"I desire to be excused from attendance on all religious services here which no longer appeal to my curiosity or sense of obligation. I need practical assistance not spiritual consolation.

"My imagination has already been overworked to the impairment of my other mental faculties.

"I do not believe in the Christian religion. I have formulated a creed agreeable to my mind.

"I have always been fearful of those to whom government grants the special privilege to furnish a particular brand of theology.

"I deny the right of government to compel me to attend any kind of religious service. I claim and proclaim my religious freedom under the U. S. constitution.
Note.

"In reformatory and penal institutions I have attended religious service every Sunday for forty odd years—*to what purpose?*"

The entire career of this unfortunate prisoner was determined by his imprisonment in his childhood, and as well might he have been sentenced for life in his cradle. The system in which he was born in poverty condemned him to a life of crime and penal servitude in which he typifies the lot of countless thousands of others doomed to a living death behind prison walls.

CHAPTER XV.

POVERTY AND THE PRISON.

There is an intimate relation between the poor-house and the prison. Both are made necessary in a society which is based upon exploitation. The aged and infirm who remain docile and submissive through the struggle for existence, to whatever straits it may reduce them, are permitted to spend their declining days in the county house and to rest at last in the pottersfield.

But they who protest against their pitiless fate rather than yield to its stern decrees, they who refuse to beg, preferring to take the chances of helping themselves by whatever means seem most available, are almost inevitably booked for the jail and the prison.

Poverty has in all ages, in every nation, and under every government recorded in history, been the common lot of the great mass of mankind. The many have had to toil and produce in poverty that the few might enjoy in luxury and extravagance. But however necessary this may have been in the past, it need no longer be true in our day.

Through invention and discovery and the application of machinery to industry, the productive forces of labor have been so vastly augmented that if society were properly organized the great body of the people, who constitute the workers and producers, instead of being poor and miserable and dependent as they now are, would be happy and free and thrill with the joy of life.

There can be no question about the simple and self-evident facts as here set forth:

First, here in the United States we live in as rich a land as there is on earth.

Second, we have all the natural resources, all the raw materials from which wealth is produced in practically unlimited abundance.

Third, we have the most highly efficient productive machinery in the world.

Fourth, we have millions of workers skilled and unskilled not only ready, but eager, to apply their labor to the industrial machinery and produce a sufficiency of all that is required to satisfy the needs and wants of every man, woman and child under a civilized standard of living.

Then why should millions be idle and suffering, millions of others toiling for a pittance, and all the victims of poverty, and of a bleak and barren existence?

The answer is, that capitalism under which we now live has outlived its usefulness and is no longer adapted to the social and economic conditions that today confront the world. Profit has precedence over life, and when profit cannot be made, industry is paralyzed and the people starve.

Here let it be said again, and it cannot be repeated too often nor made too emphatic, that poverty and ignorance, with which poverty goes hand in hand, constitute the prolific source from which flow in a steady and increasing stream most of the evils which afflict mankind.

It is poverty from which the slums, the red light district, the asylums, the jails and the prisons are mainly recruited.

It was in the so-called panic of 1873, which lasted five years and during which millions were in a state of enforced idleness due to "over production", that the "tramp" made his appearance in American life. The industrious working man, turned by his employer into the street because he had produced more goods than could be sold, became a tramp; the tramp in some instances became a beggar and in others a thief and criminal. From that time to this the tramp has been a fixed institution in American life, and epidemics of crime are reported with regularity in the daily press.

Poverty breeds misery and misery breeds crime. It is thus the prison is populated and made to prosper as a permanent and indispensable adjunct to our Christian civilization. The most casual examination of the inmates of jails and prisons shows the great majority of them at a glance to be of the poorer classes.

When, perchance, some rich man goes to prison the instance is so remarkable that it excites great curiosity and amazement. A rich man does not fit in prison. The prison was not made for him. He does not belong there and he does not stay there. The rich man goes to prison only as the exception to prove the rule.

The social system that condemns men, women and children to poverty at the same time pronounces upon many of them the sentence of the law that makes them convicts. And this social system in the United States rests on the foundation of private ownership of the social means of the common life.

Two per cent of the American people own and control the principal industries and the great bulk of the wealth of the nation. This interesting and amazing fact lies at the bottom of the industrial paralysis and the widespread protest and discontent which prevail as these lines are written. The daily papers are almost solid chronicles of vice and immorality, of corruption and crime.

In the City of Chicago the authorities frankly admit being no longer able to cope with crime and, happily, Judge W. M. Gammill, of that city, comes to the rescue by recommending the reestablishment of the whipping post as a deterrant for the crimes and misdemeanors committed by the victims of a vicious social system which Judge Gammill upholds. The distinguished judge's Christian spirit as well as his judicial mind are vindicated in his happy and thoughful suggestion which is finding ready echo among ruling class parasites and mercenaries who, no doubt, would experience great delight in seeing the poor wretches that are now only jailed for the crimes that the injustice of society forces them to commit, tied to a post and their flesh lacerated into shreds by a whip in the hands of a brute.

Commenting upon Judge Gammill's advocacy of the whipping post the Tribune of Terre Haute, the city in which I live, has the following illuminating editorial in its columns dated April 12, 1922:

THE WHIPPING POST.

"Revival of the whipping post, Judge W. M. Gammill, of Chicago, yesterday told the committee on law enforcement of the American Bar Association, would have a great effect on the reduction of crime. He cited examples where flogging tended to reduce crime and presented figures showing the number of murders in the large cities. In 1921 his figures showed that St. Louis had 26 murders; Philadelphia, 346; New York, 261; Chicago, 206; Boston, 102, and Washington, 69.

"There is a good deal to this. Mushy sentiment regarding 'honor system', and the soft theories that criminals are not criminals but sick men, and other things of this sort, have reduced the fear of the law to a minimum and desperate characters no longer hesitate at desperate crimes.

"Half-baked minds will register horror at the

idea of restoring the whipping post. These will
cry that the world is 'returning to barbarism'.
The fact is that the world can return to 'barbarism' with the forces of law and order directing the 'return', or it can return to the barbarism of the criminal, where life and property
are held at naught, and rule is by the pistol,
black-jack and terrorism. The present crime
wave indicates that the world is well on its way to
return to the latter form of 'barbarism' and the
law-abiding people of the world are getting very
much the worst of it. The general re-establishment of the whipping post would stop the present
well advanced return to barbarism. The whipping post should hold terror for but one class,
and the sooner this class is banished from our society the better. No law abiding citizens should
have any apprehension over Judge Gammill's
suggestion''.

This editorial, reflecting as it does the enlightened opinion of the ruling class of which it
is a recognized organ in the community, is its own
sufficient commentary.

In the chapter which follows I shall show how
poverty as it now exists may be abolished, and
how in consequence of such an organic social
change the prison as such would no longer be
necessary.

For the present I feel impelled to emphasize
the fact that poverty is mainly responsible for
the prison and that, after all, it is poverty that

is penalized and imprisoned under the present social order.

It is true that people may be poor and not go to prison, but it is likewise true that most of those who serve prison sentences do so as the result of their poverty.

From the hour of my first imprisonment in a filthy county jail I recognized the fact that the prison was essentially an institution for the punishment of the poor, and this is one of many reasons why I abhor the prison, and why I recognize it to be my duty to do all in my power to humanize it as far as possible while it exists, and at the same time to put forth all my efforts to abolish the social system which makes the prison necessary by creating the victims who rot behind its ghastly walls.

CHAPTER XVI.

SOCIALISM AND THE PRISON.

Socialism and prison are antagonistic terms.

Socialism means freedom and when the people are free they will not be under the necessity of committing crime and going to prison. Such exceptional cases as there may be requiring restraint for the protection of society will be cared for in institutions and under conditions betokening a civilization worthy of the name.

Socialism will abolish the prison by removing its cause and putting an end to the vicious conditions which make such a hideous thing as the prison a necessity in the community life.

I am aware in advance that what is said here in regard to abolishing the prison will be met with incredulity, if not derision, and that the theory and proposal I advance will be pronounced visionary, impractical and impossible. Nevertheless, my confidence remains unshaken that the time will come when society will be so far advanced that it will be too civilized and too humane to maintain a prison for the punishment of an erring member, and that man will think too well of himself to cage his brother as a brute, place an armed brute over him, feed him as a brute, treat him as a brute, and reduce him to the level of a brute.

Socialism proposes that the people—all the people—shall socially own the sources of wealth and social means with which wealth is produced; that the people, in other words, shall be the joint proprietors upon equal terms of the industries of the nation, that these shall be co-operatively operated and democratically managed; it proposes that the people shall appropriate to themselves the whole of the wealth they create to freely satisfy their normal wants instead of turning the bulk of that wealth over, as they now do, to idlers, parasites and non-producers while they suffer in poverty and want.

When the community life is organized upon a co-operative basis according to the socialistic program every man and woman will have the inalienable right to work with the most improved modern machinery and under the most favorable possible conditions with the assurance that they will receive in return the equivalent of their product, and that they may enjoy in freedom and peace the fruit of their labor.

In such a society there will be a mutuality of interest and a fraternity of spirit that will preclude the class antagonism and the hatred resulting therefrom which now prevail, and men and women will work together with joy, not as wage slaves for a pittance, but in economic freedom and in an atmosphere of mutual goodwill and peace. The machine will be the only slave, the workday will be reduced in proportion as the productive capacity is increased by improved machinery and methods, so that each life may be assured sufficient leisure for its higher and nobler development.

What incentive would there be for a man to steal when he could acquire a happy living so much more easily and reputably by doing his share of the community work? He would have to be a perverted product of capitalism indeed who would rather steal than serve in such a community. Men do not shrink from work, but from slavery. The man who works primarily for the benefit of another does so only under compulsion, and work so done is the very essence of slavery.

Under Socialism no man will depend upon another for a job, or upon the self-interest or good will of another for a chance to earn bread for his wife and child. No man will work to make a profit for another, to enrich an idler, for the idler will no longer own the means of life. No man will be an economic dependent and no man need feel the pinch of poverty that robs life of all joy and ends finally in the county house, the prison and pottersfield.

The healthy members of the community will all be workers, and they will be rulers as well as workers, for they will be their own masters and freely determine the conditions under which they shall work and live. There will be no arrogant capitalists on the one hand demanding their profits, nor upon the other cowering wage slaves dependent upon paltry and insufficient wages.

Industrial self-government, social democracy, will completely revolutionize the community life. For the first time in history the people will be truly free and rule themselves, and when this comes to pass poverty will vanish like mist before the sunrise. When poverty goes out of the world the prison will remain only as a monument to the ages before light dawned upon darkness and civilization came to mankind.

It is to inaugurate this world-wide organic social change that the workers in all lands and all climes are marshaling their forces, recognizing their kinship, and proclaiming their international solidarity.

The world's workers are to become the world's rulers. The great transformation is impending and all the underlying laws of the social fabric and all the irresistable forces of industrial and social evolution are committed to its triumphant consummation.

Capitalism has had its day and must go. The capitalist cannot function as such in free society. He will own no job except his own as a worker and to hold that he must work for what he gets the same as any other worker. No man has, or ever did have, the right to live on the labor of another; to make a profit out of another, to rob another of the fruit of his toil, his liberty and his life.

Capitalism is inherently a criminal system for it is based upon the robbery of the working class and corner-stoned in its slavery. The title-deed held by the capitalist class to the tools used by the working class is also the title-deed to their liberty and their lives.

Economic slavery is at the foundation of every other slavery of body, mind and soul. But the capitalists rob not only the workers, but also themselves in appropriating what is produced in the sweat and misery of their toil. They lapse into a state of parasitism that robs them of their higher development, the intellectual and spiritual estate to which all human beings are heirs who live in accordance with the higher laws of their being.

Often at night in my narrow prison quarters when all about me was quiet I beheld as in a vision the majestic march of events in the transformation of the world.

I saw the working class in which I was born and reared, and to whom I owe my all, engaged in the last great conflict to break the fetters that have bound them for ages, and to stand forth at last, emancipated from every form of servitude, the sovereign rulers of the world.

It was this vision that sustained me in every hour of my imprisonment, for I felt deep within me, in a way that made it prophecy fulfilled, that

229

the long night was far spent and that the dawn of the glad new day was near at hand.

In my prison life I saw in a way I never had before the blighting, disfiguring, destroying effects of capitalism. I saw here accentuated and made more hideous and revolting than is manifest in the outer world the effects of the oppression and cruelty inflicted upon the victims of this iniquitous system.

On the outside of the prison walls the wage slave begs his master for a job; on the inside he cowers before the club of his keeper. The entire process is a degenerating one and robs the human being, either as a wage slave walking the street or as a convict crouching in a cell, of every attribute of sovereignty and every quality that dignifies his nature.

Socialism is the antithesis of capitalism. It means nothing that capitalism means, and everything that capitalism does not.

Capitalism means private ownership, competition, slavery and starvation.

Socialism means social ownership, co-operation, freedom and abundance for all.

Socialism is the spontaneous expression of human nature in concrete social forms to meet the demands and regulate the terms of the common life.

The human being is a social being, and Socialism would organize his life in the social spirit, under social conditions and along social lines of advancement.

What more natural than that things of a social nature in a community should be socially owned and socially administered for the individual and social well-being of all!

What more unnatural, what more antagonistic to every social instinct, than the private ownership of the social means of life!

Socialism is evolving every hour of the day and night and all attempts to arrest its progress but increase its power, accelerate its momentum, and insure its triumph for the liberation of humanity throughout the world.

CHAPTER XVII.

(Addres before Nineteenth Century Club at
Delmonico's, New York City, March
21st, 1899.)

In my early years I stood before the open door
of a blazing furnace and piled in the fuel to create steam to speed a locomotive along the iron
track of progress and civilization. In the cos-
tume of my craft, through the grime of mingled
sweat and smoke and dust I was initiated into
the great brotherhood of labor. The locomotive
was my alma mater. I mastered the curriculum
and graduated with the degree of D. D., not, as
the lexicons interpret the letters, "Doctor of Divinity", but that better signification, "Do and
Dare"—a higher degree than Aristotle conferred
in his Lyceum or Plato thundered from his
academy.

I am not in the habit of telling how little I
know about Latin to those who have slaked their
thirst for learning at the Pierian springs, but
there is a proverb that has come down to us from
the dim past which reads, "Omnia vincit labor"
and which has been adopted as the shibboleth of
the American labor movement because, when re-

duced to English, it reads "Labor overcomes all things". In a certain sense this is true. Labor has built this great metropolis of the new world, built it as coral insects build the foundations of islands—build and die; build from the fathomless depths of the ocean until the mountain billows are dashed into spray as they beat against the fortifications beneath which the builders are forever entombed and forgotten.

Here in this proud city where wealth has built its monuments grander and more imposing than any of the seven wonders of the world named in classic lore, if you will excavate for facts you will find the remains, the bones of the toilers, buried and embedded in their foundations. They lived, they wrought, they died. In their time they may have laughed and sung and danced to the music of their clanking chains. They married, propagated their species, and perpetuated conditions which, growing steadily worse, are today the foulest blot the imagination can conceive upon our much vaunted civilization.

And from these conditions there flow a thousand streams of vice and crime which have broadened and deepened until they constitute a perpetual menace to the peace and security of society. Jails, work-houses, reformatories and penitentiaries have been crowded with victims, and the question how to control these institutions and their unfortunate inmates is challenging the most serious thought of the most advanced nations on the globe.

The particular phase of this grave and melancholy question which we are to consider this evening is embodied in the subject assigned the speakers "Prison Labor, Its Effect on Industry and Trade".

I must confess that it would have suited my purpose better had the subject been transposed so as to read: "Industry and Trade, Their Effect on Labor", for, as a Socialist, I am convinced that the prison problem is rooted in the present system of industry and trade, carried forward, as it is, purely for private profit without the slightest regard to the effect upon those engaged in it, especially the men, women and children who perform the useful, productive labor which has created all wealth and all civilization.

Serious as is the problem presented in the subject of our discussion, it is yet insignificant when compared with the vastly greater question of the effect of our social and economic system upon industry and trade.

The pernicious effect of prison contract labor upon "free labor", so-called, when brought into competition with it in the open market, is universally conceded, but it should not be overlooked that prison labor is itself an effect and not a cause, and that convict labor is recruited almost wholly from the propertyless, wage-working class and that the inhuman system which has reduced a comparative few from enforced idleness to crime, has sunk the whole mass of labor to the dead level of industrial servitude.

It is therefore the economic system, which is responsible for, not only prison labor, but for the gradual enslavement and degradation of all labor, that we must deal before there can be any solution of the prison labor problem or any permanent relief from its demoralizing influences.

But we will briefly consider the effects of prison labor upon industry and then pass to the larger question of the cause of prison labor and its appalling increase, to which the discussion logically leads.

From the earliest ages there has been a prison problem. The ancients had their bastiles and their dungeons. Most of the pioneers of progress, the haters of oppression, the lovers of liberty, whose names now glorify the pantheon of the world, made such institutions a necessity in their day. But civilization advances, however slowly, and there has been some progress.

It required five hundred years to travel from the inquisition to the injunction.

In the earlier days punishment was the sole purpose of imprisonment. Offenders against the ruling class must pay the penalty in a prison cell, which, not infrequently, was equipped with instruments of torture. With the civilizing process came the idea of a reformation of the culprit, and this idea prompts every investigation made of the latter-day problem. The inmates must be set to work for their own good, no less than for the good of the state.

It was at this point that the convict labor problem began and it has steadily expanded from that time to this and while there have been some temporary modifications of the evil, it is still an unmitigated curse from which there can be no escape while an economic system endures in which labor, that is to say the laborer, man, woman and child, is sold to the lowest bidder in the markets of the world.

More than thirty years ago Professor E. C. Wines and Professor Theodore W. Dwight, then commissioners of the Prison Association of New York, made a report to the legislature of the state on prison industry in which they said:

"Upon the whole it is our settled conviction that the contract system of convict labor, added to the system of political appointments, which necessarily involves a low grade of official qualification and constant changes in the prison staff, renders nugatory, to a great extent, the whole theory of our penitentiary system. Inspection may correct isolated abuses; philanthropy may relieve isolated cases of distress; and religion may effect isolated moral cures; but genuine, radical, comprehensive, systematic improvement is impossible."

The lapse of thirty years has not effected the wisdom or logic of the conclusion. It is as true now as it was then. Considered in his most favorable light, the convict is a scourge to himself, a menace to society and a burden to industry, and whatever system of convict labor may be tried, it will ultimately fail of its purpose at reformation of the criminal or the relief of industry as long as thousands of "free laborers", who have committed no crime, are unable to get work and make an honest living. Not long ago I visited a penitentiary in which a convict expressed regret that his sentence was soon to expire, where was he to go or what was he to do? And how long before he would be sentenced to a longer term for a greater crime?

The commission which investigated the matter in Ohio in 1877 reported to the legislature as follows:

"The contract system interferes in an undue manner with the honest industry of the state. It has been the cause of crippling the business of many of our manufacturers; it has been the cause of driving many of them out of business; it has been the cause of a large percentage of reductions which have taken place in the wages of our mechanics; it has been the cause of pauperizing a large portion of our laborers and in increasing crime in a corresponding degree; it has been no benefit to the state; as a reformatory measure it has been a complete, total and miserable failure; it has hardened more criminals than any other cause; it has made total wrecks morally of thousands and thousands who would have been reclaimed from the paths of vice and crime under a proper system of prison management, but who have resigned their fate to a life of hopeless degradation; it has not a single commendable feature. Its tendency is pernicious in the extreme. In short, it is an insurmountable barrier in the way of the reformation of the unfortunates who are compelled to live and labor under its evil influences; it enables a class of men to get rich out of the crimes committed by others; it leaves upon the fair escutcheon of the state a relic of the very worst form of human slavery; it is a bone of ceaseless contention between the state and its mechanical and industrial interests; it is abhorred by all and respected by none except those, perhaps, who make profit and gain out of it. It should be tolerated no longer but abolished at once.''

And yet this same system is still in effect in many of the states in the Union. The most revolting outrages have been perpetrated upon prison laborers under this diabolical system. Read the official reports and stand aghast at the atrocities committed against these morally deformed and perverted human creatures, your brothers and my brothers, for the private profit of capitalistic exploiters and the advancement of Christian civilization.

What a commentary on the capitalistic competitive system! First, men are forced into idleness. Gradually they are driven to the extremity of begging or stealing. Having still a spark of pride and self-respect they steal and are sent to jail. The first sentence seals their doom. The brand of Cain is upon them. They are identified with the criminal class. Society, whose victims they are, has exiled them forever, and with this curse ringing in their ears they proceed on their downward career, sounding every note in the scale of depravity until at last, having graduated in crime all the way from petit larceny to homicide, their last despairing sigh is wrung from them by the hangman's halter. From first to last these unfortunates, the victims of social malformation, are made the subject of speculation and traffic. The barbed iron of the prison contractor is plunged into their quivering hearts that their torture may be coined into private profit for their exploiters.

In the investigation in South Carolina, where the convicts have been leased to railroad companies the most startling disclosures were made. Out of 285 prisoners employed by one company, 128, or more than 40 per cent, died as the result, largely, of brutal treatment.

It is popular to say that society must be protected against its criminals. I prefer to believe that criminals should be protected against society, at least while we live under a system that makes the commission of crime necessary to secure employment.

The Tennessee tragedy is still fresh in the public memory. Here, as elsewhere, the convicts, themselves brutally treated, were used as a means of dragging the whole mine-working class down to their crime-cursed condition. The Tennessee Coal and Iron Company leased the convicts for the express purpose of forcing the wages of miners down to the point of subsistence. Says the official report: "The miners were compelled to work in competition with low-priced convict labor, the presence of which was used by the company as a scourge to force free laborers to its terms". Then the miners, locked out, their families suffering, driven to desperation, appealed to force and in a twinkling the laws of the state were trampled down, the authorities overpowered and defied, and almost five hundred convicts set at liberty.

Fortunately the system of leasing and contracting prison labor for private exploitation is being exposed and its frightful iniquities laid bare. Thanks to organized labor and to the spirit of prison reform, this horrifying phase of the evil is doomed to disappear before an enlightened public sentiment.

The public account system, though subject to serious criticism, is far less objectionable than either the lease, the contract or the piece price system. At least the prisoner's infirmities cease to be the prey of speculative greed and conscienceless rapacity.

The system of manufacturing for the use of state, county and municipal institutions, adopted by the State of New York, is an improvement upon those hitherto in effect, but it is certain to develop serious objections in course of time. With the use of modern machinery the limited demand will soon be supplied and then what? It may be in order to suggest that the prisoners could be employed in making shoes and clothes for the destitute poor and school books for their children and many other articles which the poor sorely need but are unable to buy.

Developing along this line it will be only a question of time until the state would be manufacturing all things for the use of the people, and then perhaps the inquiry would be pertinent: If the state can give men steady employment after they commit crime, and manufacturing can be carried forward successfully by their labor, why can it not give them employment before they are driven to that extremity, thereby preventing them from becoming criminals?

All useful labor is honest labor, even if performed in a prison. Only the labor of exploiters, such as speculators, stock-gamblers, beef-embalmers and their mercenary politicians, lawyers and other parasites—only such is dishonest labor. A thief making shoes in a penitentiary is engaged in more useful and therefore more honest labor than a "free" stonemason at work on a palace whose foundations are laid in the skulls and

241

bones, and cemented in the sweat and blood of ten thousand victims of capitalistic exploitation. In both cases the labor is compulsory. The stone-mason would not work for the trust-magnate were he not compelled to.

In ancient times only slaves labored. And as a matter of fact only slaves labor now. The millions are made by the magic of manipulation. The coal miners of West Virginia, Pennsylvania, Ohio, Indiana and Illinois receive an average wage of less than seventy-five cents a day. They perform the most useful and necessary labor, without which your homes, if possible at all, would be cheerless as caves and the great heart of industry would cease to throb. Are they free men, or are they slaves? And what is the effect of their labor on trade and industry and upon themselves and their families? Dante would search the realms of inferno in vain for such pictures of horror and despair as are to be found in the mine regions of free America.

To the student of social science the haggard fact stands forth that under the competitive system of production and distribution the prison problem will never be solved—and its effect upon trade and industry will never be greatly modified. The fact will remain that whatever labor is performed by prison labor could and should be performed by free labor, and when in the march of economic progress the capitalist system of industry for private profit succumbs to the socialist system of industry for human happiness, when the factory, which is now a penitentiary crowded with life convicts, among whom children often constitute the majority—when this factory is transformed into a temple of science, and the machine, myriad-armed and tireless, is the only slave, there will be no prison labor and the problem will cease to vex the world, and to this it is coming in obedience to the economic law, as unerring in its operation as the law of gravitation.

That prison labor, especially under the various forms of the contract system, is demoralizing in its effect on trade and industry whenever and wherever brought into competition with outside labor is, of course, conceded; but that it has been, or is at present, an especially effective factor in such demoralization is not here admitted. There is a tendency to exaggerate the blighting effect of prison labor for the purpose of obscuring the one overshadowing cause of demoralized trade and impoverished industry.

Prison labor did not reduce the miner to a walking hungerpang, his wife to a tear-stained rag, and his home to a lair. Prison labor is not responsible for the squares of squalor and the miles of misery in New York, Chicago and all other centers of population. Prison labor is not chargeable with the sweating dens in which the victims of capitalistic competition crouch in dread and fear until death comes to their rescue. Prison labor had no hand in Coeur d'Alene,

Tennesee, Homestead, Hazelton, Virdin, Pana, that suburb of hell called Pullman and other ensanguined battlefields where thousands of workingmen after being oppressed and robbed were imprisoned like felons, and shot down like vagabond dogs; where venal judges issued infamous injunctions and despotic orders at the behest of their masters, enforcing them with deputy marshals armed with pistols and clubs and supported by troops with gleaming bayonets and shotted guns to drain the veins of workingmen of blood, but for whose labor this continent would still be a wilderness. Only the tortures of hunger and nakedness provoked protest, and this was silenced by the bayonet and bullet; by the club and the blood that followed the blow.

Prison labor is not accountable for the appalling increase in insanity, in suicide, in murder, in prostitution and a thousand other forms of vice and crime which pollute every fountain and contaminate every stream designed to bless the world.

Prison labor did not create our army of unemployed, but has been recruited from its ranks, and both owe their existence to the same social and economic system.

Nor are the evil effects confined exclusively to the poor working class. There is an aspect of the case in which the rich are as unfortunate as the poor. The destiny of the capitalist class is irrevocably linked with the working class. Fichte,

244

the great German philosopher, said, "Wickedness increases in proportion to the elevation of rank".

Prison labor is but one of the manifestations of our economic development and indicates its trend. The same cause that demoralized indus try has crowded our prisons. Industry has not been impoverished by prison labor, but prison labor is the result of impoverished industry. The limited time at my command will not permit an analysis of the process.

The real question which confronts us is our industrial system and its effects upon labor. One of these effects is, as I have intimated, prison labor. What is its cause? What makes it necessary? The answer is, the competitive system, which creates wage-slavery, throws thousands out of employment and reduces the wages of thousands more to the point of bare subsistence.

Why is prison labor preferred to "free labor?" Simply because it is cheaper; it yields more profit to the man who buys, exploits and sells it. But this has its limitations. Capitalist competition that throngs the streets with idle workers, capitalist production that reduces human labor to a commodity and ultimately to crime—this system produces another kind of prison labor in the form of child labor which is being utilized more and more to complete the subjugation of the working class. There is this difference: The prison laborers are clothed and housed and fed. The child laborers whose wage

245

is a dollar a week, or even less, must take care of themselves.

Prison labor is preferred because it is cheap. So with child labor. It is not a question of prison labor, or child labor, but of *cheap* labor.

Tenement-house labor is another form of prison labor.

The effects of cheap labor on trade and industry must be the same, whether such labor is done by prisoners, tenement house slaves, children or starving "hoboes".

The prison laborer produces by machinery in abundance but does not consume. The child likewise produces, but owing to its small wages, does not consume. So with the vast army of workers whose wage grows smaller as the productive capacity of labor increases, and then society is afflicted with overproduction, the result of underconsumption. What follows? The panic. Factories close down, wage-workers are idle and suffer, middle-class business men are forced into bankruptcy, the army of tramps is increased, vice and crime are rampant and prisons and work-houses are filled to overflowing as are sewers when the streets of cities are deluged with floods.

Prison labor, like all cheap labor, is at first a source of profit to the capitalist, but finally it turns into a two-edged sword that cuts into and destroys the system that produces it.

First, the capitalist pocket is filled by the employment of cheap labor—and then the bottom drops out of it.

In the cheapening process, the pauperized mass have lost their consuming power.

The case may now be summed up as follows:

First. Prison labor is bad; it has a demoralizing effect on capitalist trade and industry.

Second. Child labor, tenement house and every other form of cheap labor is bad; it is destructive of trade and industry.

Third. Capitalist competition is bad; it creates a demand for cheap labor.

Fourth. Capitalist production is bad; it creates millionaires and mendicants, economic masters and slaves, thus intensifying the class struggle.

This indicates that the present capitalist system has outlived its usefulness, and that it is in the throes of dissolution. Capitalism is but a link in the chain of social and economic development. Just as feudalism developed capitalism and then disappeared, so capitalism is now developing socialism, and when the new social system has been completely evolved the last vestige of capitalism will fade into history.

The gigantic trust marks the change in production. It is no longer competitive but co-operative. The same mode of distribution, which must inevitably follow, will complete the process.

Co-operative labor will be the basis of the new social system, and this will be for use and not for profit. Labor will no longer be bought and sold. Industrial slavery will cease. For every man there will be the equal right to work with every other man and each will receive the fruit of his labor. Then we shall have economic equality. Involuntary idleness will be a horror of the past. Poverty will relax its grasp. The army of tramps will be disbanded because the prolific womb which now warms these unfortunates into life will become barren. Prisons will be depopulated and the prison labor problem will be solved.

Each labor-saving machine will lighten the burden and decrease the hours of toil. The soul will no longer be subordinated to the stomach. Man will live a complete life, and the march will then begin to an ideal civilization.

There is another proverb which the Latin race sent ringing down the centuries which reads, "Omnia vincit amor", or "Love conquers all things". Love and labor in alliance, working together, have transforming, redeeming and emancipating power. Under their benign sway the world can be made better and brighter.

Isaiah saw in prophetic vision a time when nations should war no more—when swords should be transformed into plowshares and spears into pruning hooks. The fulfillment of the prophecy only awaits an era when Love and Labor, in holy alliance, shall solve the economic problem.

Here, on this occasion, in this great metropolis with its thousand spires pointing heavenward, where opulence riots in luxury which challenges hyperbole, and poverty rots in sweatshops which only a Shakespeare or a Victor Hugo could describe, and the transfer to canvas would palsy the hand of a Michael Angelo—here, where wealth and want and woe bear irrefutable testimony of deplorable conditions, I stand as a socialist, protesting against the wrongs perpetrated upon Les Miserables, and pleading as best I can for a higher civilization.

The army of begging Lazaruses, with the dogs licking their sores at the gates of palaces, where the rich are clothed in purple and fine linen, with their tables groaning beneath the luxuries of all climes, make the palaces on the highlands where fashion holds sway and music lends its charms, a picture in the landscape which, in illustrating disparity, brings into bolder relief the hut and the hovel in the hollow where want, gaunt and haggard, sits at the door and where light and plenty, cheerfulness and hope are forever exiled by the despotic decree of conditions as cruel as when the Czar of Russia orders to his penal mines in Siberia the hapless subjects who dare whisper the sacred word liberty—as cruel as when this boasted land of freedom commands that a far-away, innocent people shall be shot down in jungle and lagoon, in their bamboo huts, because they dream of freedom and independence.

These conditions are as fruitful of danger to the opulent as they are of degradation to the poor. It is neither folly nor fanaticism to assert that the country cannot exist under such conditions. The higher law of righteousness, of love and labor will prevail. It is a law which commands itself to reasoning men, a primal law enacted long before Jehovah wrote the decalog amidst the thunders and lightnings of Sinai. It is a law written upon the tablets of every man's heart and conscience. It is a law infinitely above the creeds and dogmas and tangled disquisitions of the churches—the one law which in its operations will level humanity upward until men, redeemed from greed and every debasing ambition, shall obey its mandates and glory in its triumph.

Love and labor will give us the Socialist Republic—the Industrial Democracy—the equal rights of all men and women, and the emancipation of all from the cruel and debasing thraldoms of past centuries.

CHAPTER XVIII.

STUDIES BEHIND PRISON WALLS.

(Reproduced from the Century Magazine for July, 1922, by Courtesy of Its Publishers.)

The prison has a place peculiarly and entirely its own among the institutions of human society. It is there that the human being is detached from his former associations and isolated under rigorous discipline to expiate his alleged offence against society. It is the one place to which men go only under compulsion and in humiliation and shame.

When I was a boy the very word penitentiary had a shocking effect upon my sensibilities, and of course I did not dream that I would ever serve a sentence as a convicted felon within its walls. I had never seen a penitentiary, but I had seen the filthy county jail in the town in which I lived, and through its barred windows I saw the imprisoned victims and heard their foul and damning imprecations.

This gave me some idea of what the penitentiary must be like and I wondered even then if it were not possible to deal with our erring fellow men in a more humane way than by committing them into foul dungeons and treating them as if they were beasts instead of human beings.

Later in life when I had become active in the labor movement and had a part in the strikes and other disturbances of organized workers, in the course of which the leaders were not infrequently arrested and sent to jail, I came to realize that the prison could be used for purposes other than confining the criminal; used as a club to intimidate working men and women after their leaders had already been incarcerated; used as a silencer upon any expression of opinion that might not happen to be in accord with the administrative power.

So, I understood from the beginning that all men who were sent to jails and penitentiaries were not criminals; indeed, I have often had cause to think that the time may come in the life of any man when he would consider it necessary to go to prison if he would be true to the integrity of his own soul, and loyal to his inherent, God-given sovereignty as a human being. Such thoughts would come to me after my many visits to jails and penitentiaries to call upon friends and associates in the labor struggle incarcerated there.

It was in the railroad strike of 1877 that I had my first experience in seeing my associates in the railroad union sent to jail, and I began to realize that if I continued my activity I might some day go there myself. Less than twenty years later I had my first interior view of the jail as an inmate, and this experience awakened in me a keen interest in the prison and its victims. The penal question has been to me an absorbing study ever since.

The notorious old Cook County jail in Chicago, for years the choicest picking for grafting politicians, reeking with vermin and infested with sewer rats, comes vividly to memory as these lines are written. It was there that I was initiated into the moralities and mysteries of prison life. I saw at a glance what that filthy pen meant to the unfortunate creatures confined there, and at once my sympathy was quickened, and I felt myself drawn to them by a fellow feeling which grew stronger with the passing years.

Soon afterward I was sentenced to the McHenry County jail in Woodstock, Illinois, to serve a term of six months upon the charge of contempt of court for the violation of an injunction issued by the federal court during the great Pullman strike in 1894. I had pleaded in vain for a jury trial.

Fortunately for me and my convicted associates of the American Railway Union, the filthy Cook County jail was over populated at the time we were sentenced, in consequence of which we were transferred to the county jail in Woodstock. The farmers in that vicinity did not relish the idea of my being "boarded" among them even as an inmate of their jail. They had been reading the daily newspapers and had concluded that I was too dangerous a criminal to be permitted to enter the county, and it was reported that they would gather in numbers at the station on my arrival and attempt to lynch me, or at least prevent me from disembarking. When we arrived at Woodstock a number of them were at the station, but they had evidently been advised against carrying out their enthusiastic program for they made no hostile demonstration.

The jail at Woodstock was a small affair and clean for a county lock-up. I soon had a satisfactory understanding with the sheriff, a veteran of the civil war, and got along without the least trouble. During the latter period of my term I conducted an evening school for the benefit of the prisoners, and on my leaving they presented me with a set of resolutions expressive of their gratitude which is still a cherished testimonial in my possession.

Some years later when I was touring the country as a presidential candidate I made a special visit to Woodstock and received a great ovation from the visiting farmers and the townspeople, among whom was the sheriff who had been my jailer and had become my friend. On another occasion I was invited there to address a meeting at the City Hall, the daughter of the sheriff, head of the Relief Corps of the G. A. R., having charge of the arrangements.

Almost twenty-five years passed before I had my next prison experience. The world war was in progress and the excitement was intense. I had my own views in regard to the war, and I knew in advance that an expression of what was in my heart would invite a prison sentence under the Espionage Law. I took my stand in accordance with the dictates of my conscience, and was prepared to accept the consequences without complaint. The choice was deliberately made, and there has never since been a moment of regret. It was not because I yearned for imprisonment that I took the position that human beings had a higher call and a nobler purpose in life than slaughtering each other and hating those they could not kill, but simply because I could take no other, although realizing fully that the choice led through prison gates.

A sentence of ten years followed my trial at Cleveland in which I permitted no witnesses to testify in my behalf and no defense to be made. When the government's attorneys were satisfied that they had concluded their case against me, I addressed the jury, not as a matter of defense of the speech that had resulted in my arrest, trial and conviction, but in an attempt to amplify and supplement it so that there could be no possible mistake as to my beliefs and opinions with respect to the subject in controversy. It was an unusual and surprising proceeding in a courtroom. I was entirely prepared to receive the sentence of ten years pronounced by the judge. I had stood upon my constitutional right of free speech, and in this attitude I had the sanction and support of tens of thousands of people who had no sympathy with my political views.

On the evening of April 13, 1919, I was delivered by United States Marshal Lap and his deputies of Cleveland to Warden Joseph Z. Terrell, of the West Virginia State Penitentiary at Moundsville to enter upon my sentence. I was permitted to serve but two months at Moundsville when the order came from Washington for my transfer to Atlanta Federal Prison. My brief sojourn at Moundsville was entirely satisfactory as a prison experience, for after my arrival there I was introduced to the various officials and came into intimate and pleasant contact with all the prisoners.

These experiences were preliminary to my adventure at the United States Penitentiary in Atlanta, where I was taken on June 14, 1919, and served as an inmate until Christmas Day, 1921.

With this introductory sketch I shall now enter upon the story of my actual prison life and my study of the prison as an institution, the inmates confined there, the rules and conditions under which they serve their terms, and the effect of their prison experience upon their subsequent lives.

Personally, I feel amply rewarded for the opportunity that was given me to see and know the prison as it is, for while I was a prisoner at Atlanta I learned more of a vital nature to me than could have been taught me in any similar period in the classroom of any university.

A prison is a wonderful place in the opportunity afforded not only to study human nature in the abstract, to examine the causes and currents of motives and impulses, but also to see yourself reflected in the caricatures of your fellow men. It is also the one place, above all others, where one comprehends the measureless extent of man's inhumanity to man.

I hate, I abominate the prison as it exists today as the most loathsome and debasing of human institutions.

Most prisons are physically as well as morally unclean. All of them are governed by rules and maintained under conditions which fit them as breeding places for the iniquities which they are supposed to abate and stamp out.

When I entered the Atlanta Prison it was on a common footing with all the rest of the prisoners. I expected no favors and would accept no privileges that were denied to others. From the moment I entered there I felt that I was among friends, for the prisoners accorded me an enthusiastic welcome which I knew was genuine on their part. I at once made up my mind that it would be my constant endeavor to serve these fellow prisoners of mine in every way that I could and at every opportunity that presented itself. I was not there long before I realized that my attitude toward the convicts was understood by them and reciprocated in ways that shall always remain in my memory in tender testimony of the human fellowship that can blossom even in a prison if nourished by kindness of heart.

When I was put into a second-hand prison suit of blue denim I felt myself one with every prisoner in Atlanta. During the first two months I was placed in a cell which was already inhabited by five other convicts, and these inmates did everything that human beings could possibly do to make me comfortable and my stay a pleasant one. They were constantly seeking ways and means to share with me whatever they had, and from these simple souls I learned something about unselfishness, and thoughtfulness, and respect for another's feelings—qualities that are not too common in the outer world where men are more or less free to practice them without being watched by brutal guards with clubs in their hands eager to proclaim their authority with the might of the bludgeon.

We sat side by side and ate the same wretched food together, and after our evening meal in the general mess we spent fourteen consecutive hours together locked in a steel cage. I found my cellmates to be just as humane as any men I had ever met in the outer world.

I have heard people refer to the "convict countenance". I never saw one. The rarest of human beings, the most cultured and refined amongst us might in time become brutal by the blighting and brutalizing influence of the prison if they should permit themselves to yield their spirit to the degrading and debasing atmosphere that permeates every penitentiary in the land.

By far the most of my fellow prisoners were poor and uneducated men who never had a decent chance in life to cultivate the higher arts of humanity, but never in all the time I spent among those more than 2,000 convicts did one of them give me an unkind word.

There is infinite power in human kindness. Every one of those convicts without a single exception responded in kindness to the touch of kindness. I made it my especial duty to seek out those who were regarded as the worst specimens, but I never found one who failed to treat me as decently as I treated him. My code of conduct toward my fellow prisoners had the same efficacy in prison that it had elsewhere. In dealing with human beings I know no race, no color and no creed. At the roots I think we are all alike, governed by similar impulses that have more or less the same results, depending upon the circumstances in which we find ourselves placed, and considering the conditions that attend us. I judge not and I try to treat others as I would be treated by them.

But in prison the human element is sadly discounted and men are made by cruel and senseless rules to fit into the criminal conceptions of them which prevail under the prison regime.

The prison, above all others, should be the most

259

human of institutions. A great majority of the inmates are there because of their poverty and the direct or indirect results of poverty. Their misfortune in life is penalized and they are branded as convicts for the rest of their lives.

If an intelligent study could be made of each individual case in a federal or state prison and the result truthfully placed before the people the nation would be horrified at the cruel injustice which would be revealed. Most of the victims of prison injustice are without friends of influence to intercede in their behalf, and society in the aggregate has no concern in them whatsoever.

The average prison is in the control of politicians who know little and care less about what takes place behind the walls. Prison officials are placed in responsible positions to reward them for their political services and not with reference to either their character or qualifications for the office.

The warden and deputy warden of a prison should have exceptional qualities to fit them for the discharge of their important duties, and they should be among the most humane of men.

One of the first things I discovered in Atlanta prison was the wretched food provided for the prisoners and the disgusting manner in which it was cooked and served. The menu was confined to a few poor articles which palled upon the appetite and was the source of universal daily complaint and dissatisfaction.

Soon after I entered prison the question occurred to me: why are men who work here not paid
for their labor? They are here under punishment for having stolen perhaps a few dollars and
promptly upon their incarceration the government
or the state proceeds to rob them of their daily
earnings, compelling them to work day after day
without a cent of compensation. The service
which the state exacts from a convict should be
paid for at the prevailing rate of wages to be
placed to his credit on the books, or shared with
his family, so that on leaving the prison he would
not have to face a hostile world in a shoddy suit
of clothes and $5.00 in his pocket as his sole capi-
tal with which to start life anew.

The clubs and guns in the hands of guards
present a picture well calculated to reveal the
true character of the prison as a humanizing and
redeeming institution.

As a matter of fact, the prison is simply a re-
flex of the sins which society commits against
itself. The most thorough study of prison inmates that I was able to make in the course of
my intimate daily and nightly contact with thousands of them convinced me beyond all question
that they are in all essential respects the same
as the average run of people in the outer world.
I was unable to discover the criminal type or the
criminal element of which I had heard and read
so much before I had the opportunity to make
my own investigation. That there are moral and

mental defectives in prison is of course admitted, but the number is not greater, nor are the cases more pronounced, than may be found outside of prison walls.

However, in dealing with these imprisoned and helpless beings in the prevailing prison spirit and under the omnipresent iron clad regulations, they must necessarily be regarded as a dangerous and vicious aggregation in order to justify the brutal and corrupt system which, under the pretense of reformation, preys upon their misfortune. There are many flagrant abuses and evils in the present prison regime and these have their source and incentive primarily in being in the control of politicians who wax fat out of the misery of convicts by delivering them, in many states, to heartless contractors who in turn sweat and rob them, not only of their labor but of their health and very lives. The prison labor contractor is the most merciless of slave-drivers.

I have seen enough of this shocking cruelty to forever damn the institution in which such an outrage upon unfortunates is practiced. In the matter of convict labor the state virtually sells its outcast citizens into abject slavery so that thieving contractors, the pals of politicians who control the prison, may fatten upon the proceeds of their crimes against so-called criminals.

Are the vultures who thus prey upon the helpless, robed as they are in the soft raiment of respectability, not actually lower morally than the victims of their inhumanity and piracy? And if men should be sent to prison for robbery, are not these official mercenaries the very creatures who, instead of controlling the prison, should themselves be under its own brutal regulations?

That the vicious and corrupting abuses herein set forth were recognized years ago by men who honestly attempted to correct them is clearly stated in a report to the New York State Legislature issued more than half a century ago by Professor E. C. Wines and Professor Theodore W. Dwight, then Commissioners of the Prison Association of New York, from which I quote as follows:

"Upon the whole it is our settled conviction that *the contract system of convict labor, added to the system of political appointments,* which necessarily involves a low grade of official qualification and constant changes in the prison staff, renders nugatory, to a great extent, the whole theory of our penitentiary system. Inspection may correct isolated abuses; philanthropy may relieve isolated cases of distress; and religion may effect isolated moral cures; *but genuine, radical, comprehensive, systematic improvement is impossible.*" (Italics are mine).

As long as the prison is in control of politicians and under the supervision of their creatures, its callous indifference to the inmates, its internal vices and abuses, and its external reaction in furnishing society with a steady stream of criminals trained in its own institution will continue, and isolated instances of superficial improvement will not materially reduce the evil and corrupting power.

I am not at all inclined to exploit my personal prison experience and should prefer to omit that element entirely, were it not necessary to the purpose of this article to include some reference to it. It is to be doubted if there was ever before in prison history a case parallel to my own in point of experience and results issuing therefrom.

I had been four times the candidate for President of the United States of the party representing the class toiling in penury and suffering from whose ranks are recruited, under the lash of poverty and misery, with but few exceptions, the victims of penal misrule. Since my early boyhood, and practically through my entire life, I had been in intimate association with working people and those who are generally regarded as the "lower class". My understanding of their conditions, my perception of the basic social causes that had preceded their predicament, and my sympathy with them even in their transgressions, which is usually the result of their wretched lot, had preceded my entrance through the prison gates.

The entire prison seemed to join in the sympathetic reception accorded me. The question was frequently asked, sometimes sneeringly by the guards, and sometimes in a spirit of wonder and admiration, by what magic I held the interest of my fellow prisoners and won their affection and devotion. The answer is a quite simple one. I recognized in each of them my brother and treated him accordingly. I did not moralize or patronize my fellow convicts in the least. Men who are caged and watched, spied upon and hunted like animals develop certain latent instincts that become amazingly keen and discerning. Among these is the instinct to divine what is in the heart of those who approach them. They have been robbed of their respectability and forever denied the chance to regain it, and, sensitive as they surely are to this circumstance, they are not apt to be impressed by those who pose before them as their moral superiors.

They recognize no redeeming influence in moralizing rebuke. They resent being patronized, even the most ignorant of them, unless in the prison atmosphere they have degenerated into stool pigeons. No one who *condescends* to serve these prisoners can win their graces or exercise any salutary influence upon them. They hunger for sympathy, but it must be genuine, human, warm from the heart.

The late Father Michael J. Byrne, of the federal prison at Atlanta, was in all respects the finest prison chaplain I have ever known. I had no church affiliation, and for reasons of my own I rarely attended devotional exercises at the chapel, but I loved Father Byrne and we would talk together many hours in my little room in the prison hospital.

Devotional offerings in the name of the merciful Jesus, who loved the poor and freely forgave their sins, on an altar presided over by grim visaged guards with clubs in their clutches ready to fell the worshippers was not compatible with my sense of religious worship. Before I entered Atlanta prison attendance at chapel was compulsory. Almost from the start I declined to go myself, partly because of the hideous mockery which the scene and setting made of sincere worship, and I think that as a result of my resolute protest the rule was modified and attendance became voluntary, but the guards with clubs in their fists remained.

Father Byrne ministered in the spirit of loving service to all alike, no matter how low some might seem in the eyes of others, and that is why he and I instantly became friends and co-operated with each other to the full extent that my restrictions as a convict would allow. It may seem strange, but it is nevertheless true, that not only do the prison rules not counternance inmates being kind and helpful to each other, but on the contrary, they forbid their being so, and encourage their spying upon, betraying and hating one another so that all may the more readily be kept in subjection.

In the prison hospital an inmate may be dying, but the rules forbid him being visited by his fellow prisoners; each convict must keep to himself no matter how great may be his desire to clasp the hand of a fellow prisoner whose affection he may have won in the course of their suffering and struggling together against the cruel and senseless regulations. This is one of the prison rules that I confess violating with impunity. I should have preferred going to the dungeon, known in prison parlance as "the hole", on bread and water, rather than to have obeyed that rule. As a matter of fact, nearly every prison rule is violated by every convict who stays any length of time in prison. If he would remain a human being he must of necessity break the rules in order to live. Men cannot, and will not, be unsocialized even in a prison whose rules attempt to wreck and ruin human character and personality in the quickest possible time by the harshest possible methods. But the group psychology prevails, and the rules go by the board, though often at the expense of great suffering on the part of those who transgress them.

Almost every prisoner who came to the hospital expressed an immediate desire to have me come and see him. Invariably I did so as soon as possible. I was able in many ways by voluntary ministration to ease their suffering and brighten their wretched days. Father Byrne observed a remarkable change in the moral atmosphere of the hospital after I entered there. Men no longer used foul language or told smutty stories. The relation between the guards and inmates had completely changed. It was as if the hospital building was now occupied by a harmonious human family instead of a lot of sullen and incorrigible convicts.

Both the warden and his deputy commented on the change which none appreciated more than Father Byrne.

A visiting reporter once asked Father Byrne how it was that I held such moral power over the prisoners. His answer was: "He just loves them; he talks to them and then they're different. There is something about him that wins and changes them". There is nothing mysterious or occult about the "something" to which Father Byrne referred. It was merely an active manifestation of human kindness which all of us possess, but which we are prone to smother beneath a crust of indifference to the suffering of our fellow men.

The day before the death of this noble-spirited chaplain he sent me a beautiful and touching telegram congratulating me upon my release from prison. The message read: "Heartiest congratulations and well wishes from your best friend. God bless you. Michael J. Byrne, Catholic Chaplain, U. S. Penitentiary." Father Byrne is at rest. His memory will be cherished by the thousands of convicts to whom he gave himself as freely and ministered as lovingly as the Nazarene Himself might have done in his place.

Love and service constitute the magical touchstone; they are, when fully developed and truly expressed, one and inseparable, and more imperatively needed in prison than in any other place on earth.

There is where Jesus Christ would be His perfect self in tender and sympathetic ministration, and He would require neither guns nor clubs to protect His person from insult or assault.

It is when men are most prosperous in their individual pursuits that they are more apt to be thoughtless and indifferent to the fate of others, but when they are plunged into a common abyss of misery and suffering they are likely to become sympathetic and responsive to the touch of kindness, and there is more redemptive influence in a word of love and sympathy than in all the harsh rules ever devised and all the brutal clubs ever wielded to enforce them.

There was never a moment of mine in Atlanta prison that was not mortgaged in advance. Many of the prisoners could neither read nor write, and they would come to me to have me read and answer their letters, or to fill out their blanks for pardon, parole or commutation, although much of this had to be done by stealth as it was in violation of the rules, and was several times arbitrarily forbidden by the guards, especially when prisoners were caught leaving my room. I heard their sad stories, listened in sympathy to their tragic appeals, placed my hand on their shoulders and counselled them as an elder brother, and while I was able to do but a mere trifle of what my heart would have done for them, I sensed the appreciation and gratitude that embraced the entire body of prisoners of all colors, creeds and conditions.

The scene that occurred upon my release when these 2,300 prison victims clothed as convicts, yet with human hearts throbbing beneath their tatters, spontaneously burst their bonds, as it were, rushed to the fore of the prison on all three of its floors and crowded all the barred window spaces with their eager faces, cheering while the tears trickled down their cheeks—this scene can never be described in words, nor can it ever be forgotten by those who witnessed that extraordinary and unparalleled demonstration.

In that brief moment prison rules were stripped of their restraining power, and men though in prison fetters gave lusty expression to their beautiful human impulses. It was the most deeply touching and impressive moment and the most profoundly dramatic incident of my life. Men and women on the prison reservation, including the officials who bore witness to that unusual scene, stood mute in their bewilderment. Never before had such a thing occurred, and never in the widest stretch would it have been deemed possible.

There was a reason for this unheard of demonstration, and it was not all of a personal nature. I arrogate to myself no importance whatever on account of having won the friendship of these convicts. They did vastly more for me than I was able to do for them, and the only point I make in this connection is that if the prison were conducted in the spirit and with the understanding that we convicts had for each other the whole penal system would at once be revolutionized; instead of being a bastile for debasing and destroying the unfortunate it would become in the true sense a boon to society as a reclamatory and redemptive institution.

The prison as a prison in the common acceptance of that term will always be a tragic failure. It is not only anti-social, but anti-human, and at best is bad enough to reflect the ignorance, stupidity and inhumanity of the society it serves. But this is not to say that improvement of the prison while it lasts should be discouraged. On the contrary, until the time comes when social offenders are placed under scientific treatment instead of being punished as criminals, every effort should be put forth to improve the moral and physical condition of our county jails, our state prisons and our federal penitentiaries.

For myself, I heartily commend all that is being done to arouse the people to a consciousness of the festering evils which now thrive in these places. There needs to be created a public sentiment that realizes that for its own self-protection the community must clean up the prison as far as that may be possible and make it a place where criminal tendencies may be checked and overcome instead of being encouraged and confirmed as they now are to the ruin of their immediate victims, and their increasing detriment to society.

Space will not permit more than a brief summary of the fundamental changes required to humanize the prison.

First of all, it should be taken out of the hands of politicians and placed under the supervision and direction of a board of the humanest of men with vision and understanding. This board should have absolute control, including the power of pardon, parole and commutation. Such a board as this would at all times be in immediate touch with the prisoners and have intimate knowledge of prison conditions and possibilities for improvement.

The contract system, wherever it prevails, is an unmitigated curse and should be summarily abolished.

Prison inmates should be paid for their labor at the prevailing rate of wages which should be placed to their credit in the books of the institution or shared with their families so that when the convict is released he will not have to return to a sundered home and face a hostile world.

Not a gun nor a club should be in evidence inside the walls.

The prisoners themselves, at least 75 per cent of whom are dependable, as every honest warden will admit, should be organized upon the basis of self-government and have charge of the prison, select their own subordinate officers, their own guards, their shop and other foremen; establish their own rules and regulate their own conduct under the supervision of the prison board.

Under such an organization the morale of the prison would at once improve, the spirit of the prison would be humanized, there would be better discipline, more incentive to work, and better results in every way, and all at a greatly reduced expense to the community.

There will be men to challenge these proposals as visionary, if not vicious, but I would prefer nothing more than the opportunity to vindicate my faith in human nature by being permitted, without any pecuniary compensation, to make such a demonstration.

CHAPTER XIX.

Wasting Life.

(Reproduced from the World Forum for August, 1922, by Courtesy of Its Publishers.)

If there is any surer way, any more effective method of wrecking manhood and wasting human life than our present penal system affords, the satanic thing has not come to my attention.

Six months have passed since I left that dismal cemetery of the living dead, the United States Penitentiary at Atlanta, and yet I see as vividly and appealingly as they appeared the day of my departure, the pallid faces of my fellow-prisoners pressed wistfully against the steel-barred windows of those gloomy catacombs.

The weary tramp of that mournful procession of convicts marching silently, solemnly, interminably, back and forth, back and forth, still echoes dolefully in my ears and I shall hear, like muffled drumbeats, the shuffling footfalls of that spectral prison host to the last hours of my life.

What deliberate destruction, what senseless sacrifice, what tragic and appalling waste of human life!

If life, human life, is the most precious thing in the world, then the punitive prison pen is the most wicked thing in the world, for it blasts and ruins, pollutes and destroys the lives that are committed to its pestilential moral and physical atmosphere.

I have seen boys in their teens confirmed perverts and degenerates after a few weeks in one of those penal incubators of depravity and crime.

And I have concluded in the light of my personal observation of what the penitentiary does to the young that I would rather plead guilty to murder than to putting a boy in a penitentiary for some trifling offence and branding him a convict for life.

As a rule only the poor go to prison. The rich control the courts and the poor populate the prisons.

Morgan and Rockefeller are strictly law-abiding. The hundreds of millions produced by others flow into their coffers through legal channels. They would scorn to steal. They want only what is coming to them and they and their retainers and mercenairies see that they get it and that it keeps coming. As good Christians these eminent gentlemen believe the jail the proper place for the wretch who steals rather than starve at honest work or hunting a job.

The wholesale robber acts safely within the law of his own making; the legalized looter is eminently respectable, but the petty larceny thief is a despised criminal and is properly sent to jail.

During the late war the government of the United States was robbed openly, brazenly of billions of dollars by the patriotic profiteers and contractors who precipitated the war for the loot it would yield them, but no one in his right mind expects one of them to be sent to the penitentiary.

The combined stealings and robberies of all the thieves, burglars, safe-blowers and highwaymen in the penitentiary at Atlanta would be but a trifle compared to the loot of a single profiteer and this explains why the former are convicted felons and the latter eminent patriots and philanthropists.

There is a strong incentive to steal in a system in which the great fortunes are uniformly achieved through monopolized privilege and legalized spoliation while the hardest kind of useful work yields but a wretched subsistence.

In this system almost anything pays better than honest work and useful service, and what more natural than that men should seek the "easier way" to get a living? And what more inevitable than that the deluded victims should land in a ghastly prison-house, caged like animals, for the "protection of society"?

If there is any one thing settled beyond question in criminology it is that the criminal, so-called, is the product of society, and in caging him like a beast, society in its blindness and brutality but bruises the body and scars the soul of its ill-fated offspring in punishment for its own sins.

In the nearly four years I spent among them

as a fellow-convict I came to know the inmates of prisons intimately enough to believe in them as human beings; to be convinced that as a whole they are far more sinned against than sinning, and to be willing to cast my lot with them as against the social cruelty and misunderstanding of which they are the victims.

The following pregnant paragraph quoted from Lascussagne denotes keen insight and scientific understanding, and challenges serious consideration:

"The social environment is the cultural medium of criminality; the criminal is the microbe— an element that becomes important only when it finds a medium which will cause it to ferment. EVERY SOCIETY HAS THE CRIMINALS IT DESERVES".

This means that society will have its criminals to deal with, and that the evil will become more and more costly and menacing, until society ceases producing criminals.

The staggering cost and the appalling menace to society from that source were set forth in startling terms in a treatise on "Crimes and Criminals" published by Dr. Lydston twelve years ago. The following summary is taken from a magazine review of that work by Charles Erskine Scott Wood:

"Probably the most astonishing conclusion reached in the study of this book is that society must alter its cold and brutal indifference to crime and criminals or it will be devoured by criminals just as the invisible germ of consumption devours the strong body. It is not so much a matter of humanity and sentiment as it is one of self-preservation. Dr. Lydston shows that though the population of the United States increased only 170 per cent from 1850 to 1890, crime increased 450 per cent. After making allowance for the tendency of legislatures to declare more and more crimes there still remains a vast increase of crime out of proportion to increased population. Professor Charles J. Bushnell of Washington, D. C., says it is slowly driving us toward bankruptcy, and calculates that the United States is spending as a people *Six Billions a Year* in its wrestle with crime. Professor Lydston puts it at only five billions. But five billions on the machinery to cope with crime is enough to make even the thoughtless think. Professor Lydston admits, too, that the sum spent in private detective and other unrecorded channels probably greatly swells the total. We are crazy to spend billions on armies and navies— to encourage ourselves into war—but we give no heed to the mortal disease in our midst. In war, not criminals are killed off, but the flower of the young men, leaving the degenerates in greater proportion than ever".

This showing from an authoritative source leaves no room for doubt that our method or lack of method in dealing with crime and criminals is not only an unmitigated failure but is itself a crime that indicts our social system and impeaches our civilization. And this is especially true of the penitentiary in which society avenges itself on its helpless victims by branding them as convicts, ofttimes for trivial offences, shutting them out from the world, locking them up in steel cages at the mercy of brutal keepers with clubs and guns to insult and intimidate them, to break their spirit, and destroy their manhood and self-respect.

At least seventy-five per cent of the inmates of every prison are not criminals but have simply been unfortunate, and every decent warden will admit that they would at once retrieve themselves if given their liberty and a fair chance to make good in the world. But instead they are held in deadening capitivity year after year, cut off from family and friends, branded and ostracised, compelled to subsist upon wretched if not rotten food, their natural instincts repressed, their pride insulted, and outraged until they are diseased, perverted, crazed, wrecked in body and mind, and to what purpose that does not mock and blaspheme the Author of their being?

I have made the statement and I repeat it here that if every jail, every prison, every penitentiary in the land had its doors flung wide open and every inmate were given his liberty the harm that would result to society would be vastly less than the harm society now suffers in wasting the lives of hundreds of thousands of unfortunate souls, breaking up their homes, wrecking their families, and launching upon itself the avenging crime waves which threaten it with destruction.

It is a pity indeed that the judge who puts a man in the penitentiary does not know what a penitentiary is. No one knows or can know but the inmate. See his crushed spirit, look into his troubled heart, if you can, and you may have some conception of what a penitentiary is, for there is where it leaves its deadly and everlasting mark.

Some of the finest men I ever met are behind the bars of the Moundsville prison and the Atlanta penitentiary as convicted felons. The story of each would make a volume of tragedy. The fates conspired to place them where they are. They are anything but criminals. I would rather be in their rough prison shoes than in the polished foot gear of the judges who sent them there.

In the years I spent in prison I associated freely with all the inmates without regard to color or condition. I made it a point to seek out the ones known as the worst among them, and never in a single instance in all that time was I given the least offence or did I hear an unkind word from their lips. I looked upon them all as my brothers and fellow men and treated them accordingly, and they uniformly treated me in the same way. The poorest among them were happy to have me share whatever scanty favor was permitted to come to them from the outside. I never saw men more sympathetic and considerate, and I know that many of them would have had their own sentences extended to see me given my liberty. Most of them, poor and hard-working, had been treated harshly all their days and were strangers to kindness and to the touch of a friendly hand. How quickly they responded to the first word of greeting, how readily they understood, and how gladly they returned kindness for kindness!

All these men want on earth, the great majority of them, is a decent chance to make their way in the world. And that is precisely what they are denied under the present savage system, the punitive spirit of which still lurks in the dark ages and disgraces our vaunted civilization.

This vast army of our fellow-beings, given their liberty, a fair opportunity and the right kind of encouragement, would at once retrieve their standing, walk the streets good citizens, do their share of useful work, support their families and educate their children, but this will never be until the people are awakened to the economic cause of the prison problem and to the stupendous waste of human life inherent in their blind and stupid attempt at reformation.

The entire prison regime is rank with its own innate putrescence. Graft permeates every pore of the system and the greasy palm of "political pull" is everywhere in evidence.

The average jail is a filthy, unsanitary den, in charge of a low grade politician, that would hardly make a decent pigsty.

The average prison is an unfit place for the detention of any human being. The rules are cruel and despotic, the food anything but nourishing, and the general conditions inhuman and demoralizing.

This does not appear in the report of the prison inspection, of course, and I know nothing in the way of farce that lays it over an average prison inspection.

Society with its usual consistency puts a man in prison for stealing and then proceeds promptly to rob him in the most shameless manner of the fruit of his labor for the benefit of some grafting contractor, while allowing his family to face starvation.

What right has the state to appropriate a man's daily earnings? To compel him to work without pay while his children are suffering for bread?

The man in prison, however, is better off, after all, than his dependent mother, wife and children. It is the family the judge sentences when he sends the man to prison.

Yes, it is the family that is penalized, punished without mercy though innocent of offence, and families without number all over this land are thus broken up and their members torn asunder, many of them to recruit the ranks of crime and the houses of shame.

All of which attests in overwhelming terms the frightful waste, the appalling destruction of human life in the present system of administering justice and dealing with offenders against the social code.

As these lines are written the report comes of a sensational scandal at my penal alma mater, the United States Penitentiary at Atlanta. A "dope ring" has been uncovered and a prison physician and a number of guards are implicated. Every effort is being made to suppress the scandal. According to the reports the "ring" furnishing the inmates with "dope" at extortionate rates, pocketing thousands of dollars for making "dope fiends" of young inmates who had not before used the drug. Let it be understood that drug addicts in large numbers are sentenced to the Atlanta penitentiary where they are supposed to be reformed of the pernicious habit. I am not surprised at the report. To make drug addicts while professing to reform them would be quite consistent with the whole abomniable prison scheme which makes criminals instead of reforming them.

If I were inclined to lock a human being in a steel cage under any circumstances I think I should make it a penitentiary offence to send a human being to a penitentiary. The man who sends another there should know in justice to both what it is himself.

In recalling some of my fellow-prisoners and contemplating their excellent character and human qualities I am reminded of a prison incident that occurred eight years ago in which I had an humble part. The noble character of a convict revealed in this incident must be my apology for placing it upon record here. There are men without number in prison, to my personal knowledge, of the same lofty character and tender sensibilities as this particular convict.

It was near the Christmas season, 1914. There was an organization know as the "Good Fellow Club" which provided toys and gifts to homeless and friendless children. A convict in a state prison at Jackson, Michigan, read of it and wrote the Club as follows:

"I don't know whether I would be considered a good fellow or not. Society has decreed that I was a bad fellow and has segregated me for a period. In spite of the fact that I transgressed the law I am being clothed and fed and taken care of while hundreds of people, especially children whose only crime is poverty, are actually suffering for bare necessities of life and through no fault of theirs are facing the Christmas season with scant hope of happiness. I am sending $2.00 which I hope you will be able to use to bring in some small measure gladness to some little one. You need have no fear of this money being tainted, for it was honestly earned at 15 cents a day. I have two little girls of my own and while I am sending them their Christmas money, I am sure they will be glad that I shared with some others less fortunate.

Yours in Christmas spirit,
INMATE 9756".

The foregoing letter came under my eye in the press dispatches of a local paper whereupon I wrote 9756 (a few years later I came near having that very number myself) as follows:

Terre Haute, Ind., December 16th, 1914.
Inmate No. 9756, Jackson, Mich.

My dear Brother:

"I do not know who you are but I have read your Christmas letter and I send you my greeting with my heart in it. You may be a convict but you are my brother and when your message came to me I was touched to tears.

There is more of the real religion of Jesus Christ in the spirit you breathe out to the world from behind your cruel prison bars than in all the orthodox sermons ever preached. You love the little children even as He loved them, and you are in prison while He was crucified. It is well that you are patient and forgiving. The world moves slowly. It may still be said: 'They know not what they do.'.

You had the misfortune to be born in a world not yet civilized. Jesus loved the erring into righteousness. His professed followers shut them out from God's sunlight and torture them into degeneracy and crime. The erring did not make themselves. God made them. Let Him judge them.

The society that sent you to prison devours its own offspring. Thousands of little children are starved, stunted and ground into dividends in the mills of mammon. It is the Christian society's

285

homeless, neglected babes to who you, one of its condemned convicts, feel moved to send the pennies coined in your own blood and agony.

What a sermon and what a rebuke!

If you ought to be in penitentiary I know not one who ought to be out.

Believe me with heart and hand your brother and fellow-man,

EUGENE V. DEBS''.

I did not know at the time this letter was written that I should soon be a convicted and numbered felon myself. But I must have anticipated my fate for I instinctively realized my kinship with the men behind the bars.

In going to prison myself I came to know them well and why they are there, and I came also to realize the moral obligation resting upon me to espouse their cause and to wage the war in their behalf against the vicious system that robbed them of their birthright, blasted their hopes and utterly wasted their lives.